CW00516156

how to go plant-based

a definitive guide for you and your family

Ella Mills, founder of

deliciously ella🌱

Ella x

yellow
kite

contents

recipes

breakfast

making life simpler

from the hob

from the oven

easy speedy lunches

family favourites

sweets

introduction

What does plant-based mean?

Before we delve into the book, it feels only right to start by defining the term plant-based. The expression was coined in the 1980s by Dr Thomas Colin Campbell, an American Professor of biochemistry at Cornell University, to describe a high-fibre, vegetable-rich diet; he later added 'wholefood' to the definition. It was created to distinguish a plant-based way of eating from a vegan or vegetarian diet, both of which predate the former, and move the emphasis from the moral, ethical or environmental considerations to the effect of nutrition on long-term health. As far as I understand, the aim was never to discount the value of those considerations, but instead to highlight the effect food has on our health and ensure that this was no longer a secondary consideration.

Nowadays the distinction between plant-based and vegan feels much more nuanced and at times hard to follow. I do, however, think the terms are less interchangeable than they often appear, and can be explained by three simple points:

1. The first is that veganism extends far beyond what you eat – it shapes many other life choices, whereas plant-based just refers to your diet.

2. The second is that veganism stems from a moral and ethical perspective, so the diet isn't necessarily designed to improve our health. As such, both a vegan and vegetarian approach to eating can include a lot of ultra-processed food; whereas I don't think a plant-based diet does. At its very essence a plant-based diet is about nourishment and enhancing human health and thus includes limited amounts of ultra-processed foods.

3. The third is that a plant-based approach is not all or nothing. The word 'based' denotes the simple fact that the diet has a strong emphasis on eating plants but – to my mind - does not have to exclude other foods entirely. I believe it refers to someone who is actively making the choice to eat a plant-based diet the majority of the time, say 80-90%, and within that the focus is on fresh, wholefood ingredients.

As a company, deliciously ella uses the term plant-based, as it best describes who we are and our mission of sharing delicious ways to feel better, to get more people to eat more plants and improve their wellbeing.

My story

Exactly 10 years ago, I changed my diet overnight, swapping my standard western diet – lots of quick, convenience foods, not much fruit and veg, which is now sadly the norm in the UK – for a wholefood, plant-based diet. The year before that, following my second year at university, I'd become very unwell, going from being a normal student to becoming housebound in a matter of months. A few months later, having spent most of that time in and out of hospital I was diagnosed with Postural

A plant-based approach is not all or nothing – it has a strong emphasis on eating plants but – to my mind - does not have to exclude other foods entirely.

Tachycardia Syndrome, a condition that affected the functioning of my autonomic nervous system. I struggled to control my heart rate and blood pressure, which meant that when I stood up my heart rate spiked to 150-180bpm (a normal heart rate is 60–100bpm), my blood pressure dropped, and I was so dizzy I felt that I couldn't move. I had chronic fatigue, brain fog, IBS, acid reflux, various other digestive issues, a host of infections, headaches and a lot of pain, alongside a growing sense of both depression and anxiety. It was a chronic, pretty much invisible, illness that meant I spent most of the next year in bed or confined to my house, taking all sorts of drugs including steroids and antacids, none of which made a tangible difference.

I was only 21 at this point and it almost destroyed me; there were many moments where I couldn't see what my future could be. It unravelled everything I knew about myself and took me to absolute rock bottom. Rock bottom, however, changed my life. I knew I couldn't continue along the trajectory I was on; I was going to give up or I was going to dig deeper than I thought I had the ability to do and find a solution. I chose the latter and began a period of research into what else could help me. This took me into the science of

nutrition, looking at the latest research on how our lifestyles and our food choices impact our health.

This was during the spring of 2012 and the world has changed dramatically since then, but a decade ago, this research felt pretty niche. The question of whether your diet could affect your health to such an extent was not at all part of the mainstream conversation about health in this country, and I was treated with a huge amount of scepticism initially. Moving away from ultra-processed foods, beginning to read ingredient labels (realising emulsifiers, preservatives and additives are everywhere), and learning to cook plant-based food sounds so normal now but that wasn't the case then. I didn't know a single vegan; the term plant-based was almost non-existent (I do remember someone saying it sounded like I'd just be munching on houseplants or cacti!); I couldn't find healthy, delicious, plant-based food anywhere and it was difficult to get friends and family on side.

There was a long-established community of thought-leading vegans and of course a religious and cultural history of vegetarianism in Hinduism, Jainism, Buddhism and Sikhism; the concept of plant-based, however, really didn't exist in the UK. The vegan recipes that I

8

found were much more focused on meat mimics, replacing the meat or fish with a vegan alternative, as opposed to sitting more within the plant-based angle, hero-ing the veggies, beans and fruits. Often these meat mimics were ultra-processed too, and therefore not what I was looking for – I wanted to transform and eat chickpeas and broccoli in a way that I hadn't really seen in the UK. So that's why I started deliciouslyella.com. I wanted to challenge myself, change the way I ate and make a healthy, natural, plant-focused diet my norm. Given it was so far from the mainstream narrative at this point in time, I did feel relatively alone in my initial quest. Sharing the recipes, however, quickly prompted a small community of curious, like-minded people to come together, as they were also looking for recipes to help them feel better. Most people had been struggling with their health and, like me, were looking to change their lifestyles to improve it. I instantly felt a deep sense of connection, which gave me the motivation and inspiration to go against the grain and continue to chase better health.

The more I learnt, however, the clearer it became that how we eat, how we move, how we sleep and how we manage our stress make up the building blocks of how we feel, both physically and mentally, and I needed to fundamentally change the way I lived. In doing that I wanted to make it easier for anyone else to do the same.

The power of a plant-based diet

In 2022 the world looks very different. Conversations around health are increasingly easy to access: there are countless podcasts, cookbooks, websites and resources on the topic. We're beginning to respect and appreciate the role that what we eat

and how we live plays in supporting our health, although it's certainly not far-reaching enough and there's a lot more we need to do. We're not harnessing the power of a healthy, plant-based – or predominantly plant-based – diet nearly as much as we could. Only 8% of children and 27% of adults are even achieving their five-a-day[1] and arguably that should sit closer to ten-a-day[2]. Instead, we're eating more and more ultra-processed food, with over 56% of food now bought in the UK and the US being classed as ultra-processed, bearing little to no resemblance to wholefood ingredients[3]. And we're seeing the consequences of our lifestyle choices come through to the extent that the World Health Organization shows 71% of all deaths around the world each year are caused by diseases linked to our lifestyles[4].

To claim a plant-based diet is the sole solution would be a huge oversimplification; that said, numerous studies show that eating more of a plant-based diet could be very beneficial, and certainly switching to a diet that celebrates fresh, nutritious food, filled with fruit and veg is the way forward. Data shows vegans report a reduced risk of high blood pressure, type 2 diabetes, total cancer incidences[5] (reduced by as much as 15%[6]), as well as lower cases of heart disease[7], reduced total cholesterol[8], and likelihood of being overweight or obese[9].

Likewise, we're seeing a growing conversation about the importance of a plant-based, or predominantly plant-based diet for environmental reasons. While this book is mainly focused on your and (if relevant) your family's health and wellbeing, we can't skirt around the fact that human health is inextricably linked to the health of our planet. Food production is one of the leading causes of global environmental change, and research paper after research paper clearly states that a plant-based diet is the way to change this, as the only diet that can sustainably produce sufficient nutrition without further environmental damage[10,11]. In the UK, vegans have half the carbon footprint of meat-eaters[12].

And while we don't need to be fully plant-based to reap the benefits, we need to make drastic changes – in the UK that means reducing our pork, beef and lamb intake by 89%, poultry by 66% and our dairy by 60%, only this level of change would stop the temperature rising above the crucial ceiling of 2°C[13].

Why there's no one-size-fits-all

I must caveat the above by saying that I'm not a fan of telling anyone what to do, and this book isn't designed to preach at you. I'm just a big believer in the fact that the why has to come before the how. From my experience, the more we understand the why – why we're constantly told to eat more vegetables, why our diet impacts our health, why our gut health, and therefore what we feed our gut, is so important – the more likely we are to feel motivated to make that change and implement the various tools that make up the how. Let's be honest, wanting to make a change and actually making the change are two very different things. The first is easy, the second is really hard and involves a practical day-to-day application, something made all the more challenging when life is busy, and we already feel pulled in a hundred directions – something I certainly relate to. That's why I want to make this as straightforward as possible.

I think making any dietary change achievable and sustainable for the long-term – because this is not a diet, it's

a way of living that supports you and your family's wellbeing – also relies on it feeling flexible, instead of it falling into a more dogmatic all-or-nothing approach. I'm not here to persuade or guilt-trip you into becoming 100% plant-based. This book is about supporting your choices and simply encouraging more – more veg, more wholefoods, more meals with friends and family, and, most of all, more of us to go more plant-based more of the time. You don't have to change absolutely everything about the way you eat today, or ever for that matter.

I said in my very first book in 2015 that you should adapt the recipes to make them work for you, and I stand by that seven years later. The only change since then is that I feel I have a better understanding of how to make our recipes work in your life. Having scaled a start-up to a medium-sized business with 50 people alongside my husband, Matthew, and become a mum of two, I know what busy looks like! I also understand the need many of us have to cook one meal for the whole family, not separate dishes for tinies and parents, or three meals for three different people. I hope those learnings spill out on to these pages and better support you.

Some of you may have been dabbling in plant-based eating for a while, others have been full time vegans for decades and some readers may be brand new to both concepts. If you are new to this or you are plant-based some of the time (a more flexitarian approach) but are looking to shift that balance in favour of plants more of the time, then it may be helpful to focus on the foundations first: how can I include more meat-free meals? How can I find more plant-based meals I enjoy? How can I get my family to embrace elements of it? How can I increase our vegetable intake, meeting the 5-10-a-day target, and get the 30g

Making any dietary change achievable and sustainable for the long-term relies on it feeling flexible, instead of it falling into a more dogmatic all-or-nothing outlook.

of daily fibre that I need (something that very few of us are doing)? Instead of how can I change everything right now?

Wherever you sit on that continuum, I just want to reiterate that it's okay to find big changes a little overwhelming to begin with. I had absolutely no idea where to start 10 years ago; there was no definitive guide and I certainly found that initially I had many more questions than answers. I really feel the current lack of clear, easy-to-follow information holds lots of us back. And it's not helped by the fact that there's so much conflicting information online and within the media. When I asked our social media community what barriers they faced when it came to changing their diets, they echoed these sentiments. A general sense of confusion was stopping many people from making the changes that they wanted in their lives. Questions like, what does a balanced meal look like? Can I do it quickly, simply and on a budget? How do I bring my friends and family into it? Where does protein come from? How about calcium, iron, zinc? What should I supplement? Are there any things to watch out for? Can children eat a plant-based diet? What about teenagers? What are the benefits? And the possible problems?

I hope this book clears this up for you, demystifying how to go plant-based. I know that the biggest barriers are a lack of time; a nervousness around what a balanced, healthy, plant-based meal looks like; a concern about costs; a question as to whether the diet will be interesting enough given it doesn't include every food group; and a lack of confidence in the kitchen. Overcoming each one of these has sat at the heart of creating this book. The book has been a huge labour of love and I'm so grateful to have worked with such an extraordinary group of people to bring it to life. This is by no means a solo endeavour and throughout the book you'll find essays and nutritional support from seven brilliant doctors, nutritionists, dieticians and psychologists, all of whom you'll meet on the next page. In that sense it's a little different from my previous cookbooks in the amount of information included, and I hope it'll really guide you and your family in your choices, allowing you to make the most informed decisions on the way you eat, and make going plant-based simpler and more delicious than it's ever felt before.

With love,
Ella x

meet the experts

Dr Shireen Kassam

Dr Gemma Newman

Dr Alan Desmond

Rosemary Martin

Rohini Bajekal

Paula Hallam

Shahroo Izadi

I've been lucky to meet an array of leading doctors, nutritionists, scientists, dieticians, psychologists and other healthcare professionals over the last 10 years. They've been instrumental in my learning so when I started putting this book together I created a list of the experts I felt would bring the knowledge and authority needed for the project. Each expert has contributed an essay on improving your health in some way, be it changing your diet and lifestyle, improving your gut health, or shifting your mindset. You'll also find their go-to recipes throughout the book, for extra inspiration. I'm very proud to have the opportunity to work with them, and I hope you'll learn as much from them as I have.

Dr Shireen Kassam
Shireen is a consultant haematologist and honorary senior lecturer with over 20 years' clinical experience in the NHS, a PhD, a series of published peer-reviewed papers, a qualification in plant-based nutrition and one in lifestyle medicine. Shireen specialises in treating patients with lymphoma (cancer of the lymphatic system). Over the last 10 years she has become increasingly passionate about promoting plant-based nutrition for the prevention and reversal of chronic diseases. In 2017 Shireen founded Plant-based Health Professionals UK, to bring evidence-based education on plant-based nutrition to the UK. She also runs Plant Based Health Online, the first multi-disciplinary, plant-based lifestyle medicine healthcare service.
plantbasedhealthprofessionals.com
@plantbasedhealthprofessionals

Dr Gemma Newman
Gemma is an NHS GP who has practised medicine for 18 years and is

the Senior Partner at a family medical practice. Gemma has worked in many specialities as a doctor, including elderly care, pediatrics, obstetrics and psychiatry. She's a mum of two boys, a founding member of Plant Based Health Professionals, a podcast host, an author and a passionate advocate for a lifestyle-centered approach to health.
gemmanewman.com
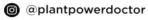 @plantpowerdoctor

Dr Alan Desmond

Dr Alan Desmond is a Consultant Gastroenterologist in the NHS who is dedicated to making evidence-based dietary advice an essential part of his practice, educating the public on the power of a wholefood, plant-based diet and the importance of good gut health. Alan completed his medical training in Ireland and Oxford and is a fellow of the Royal College of Physicians, London. He has published several influential research papers in the field of Inflammatory Bowel Disease and specialises in the role of diet in the prevention and treatment of Crohn's disease and Ulcerative Colitis.
alandesmond.com
@dr.alandesmond

Rosemary Martin BSc MSc RD (Rosie)

Rosie is a registered dietician working between the NHS and her private practice, Rosemary Nutrition & Dietetics. She specialises in plant-based nutrition, supporting others to embrace a plant-based diet for human, animal and planetary health.
rosemarynutrition.co.uk
@plantdietitianrosie

Rohini Bajekal MA Oxon MSc Dip IBLM

Rohini is a nutritionist, author and Board-Certified Lifestyle Medicine Professional. She provides one-to-one evidence-based nutrition and lifestyle advice to her clients around the world with a focus on the benefits of plant-based nutrition. She also volunteers as a cookery teacher at Made in Hackney, provides expertise around South Asian diets and leads communications at Plant-Based Health Professionals.
rohinibajekal.com
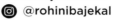 @rohinibajekal

Paula Hallam BSc (Hons) RD PG Cert

Paula is a specialist pediatric dietician with over 20 years of clinical experience, including at Great Ormond Street and Evelina Children's Hospitals. Paula specialises in empowering parents to help their children eat more plants, building on the fact that the foundations of healthy eating are laid at an early age. She now runs Tiny Tots Nutrition and Plant Based Kids and is a mum to two little girls.
tinytotsnutrition.co.uk
@tinytotsnutriton;
@plantbasedkids.uk

Shahroo Izadi

Shahroo is an award-winning Behavioural Change Specialist and psychologist. Her non-judgmental, compassion-based approach to changing habits is influenced by the experience that she gained across various roles in the addiction treatment field, including within the NHS and the Amy Winehouse Foundation. Throughout her work, Shahroo is dedicated to showing people how much easier behaviour change becomes when we learn to support, value and champion ourselves.
shahrooizadi.co.uk
@shahroo_izadi

14

our top 10 faqs

This book has been written with the deliciously ella community's contribution, looking at what our readers struggle with and their most commonly asked questions. Before we delve into the book, I wanted to address as many of these as I could. Below are the top 10 most frequently asked questions I receive about a plant-based diet.

1. What's the difference between vegan, plant-based, vegetarian and flexitarian?

The term 'vegan' was coined in 1944 by Donald Watson, an English animal rights advocate who founded The Vegan Society, to describe someone who abstained from animal products for ethical reasons. Veganism refers to your whole lifestyle, not just what's on your plate.

The term 'plant-based' was devised in the 1980s by Dr Thomas Colin Campbell, an American Professor of biochemistry at Cornell University, in reference to a high-fibre, vegetable rich diet. It was created to focus on human health rather than ethics.

A vegetarian diet has a much longer history. It was first mentioned by the Greek philosopher and mathematician Pythagoras of Samos around 500BC, with the first vegetarian society created in 1847 in England – almost 100 years before the word vegan even existed. While plant-based refers to a diet that is mostly (or entirely) made up of plant foods, a vegetarian diet includes more dairy products and eggs.

A flexitarian diet is the most recent addition to the conversation. It was coined by the American dietician Dawn Jackson Blatner in 2008. The word itself is a fusion of flexible and vegetarian, and thus refers to someone who has a primarily vegetarian diet but occasionally eats meat or fish.

Simply put it's a continuum that ladders up from absolutely no animal products in any part of your life at the vegan end, to a more flexible approach that includes lots of plants, but also animal products at the flexitarian end.

2. What does a balanced plant-based diet include? I want to start but I don't feel I have the knowledge or the confidence.

A plant-based diet focuses on fresh, wholefood, plant-based ingredients: fruits, vegetables, nuts, seeds, whole grains, beans and legumes. This list may sound a little boring when you first read it, but the reality couldn't be further from the case. In terms of ensuring it's balanced, it's the same as any diet, each meal should have a mix of complex carbohydrates, protein and healthy fats – the three together support stable blood sugar, which stops you having the spikes and crashes that leave you lethargic and craving more sweet food. To meet the vitamin and mineral needs, those meals should contain a rainbow and vary a lot throughout the week. Building a Balanced Plant-based Diet on pages 34–47 should really help you gain more confidence in creating a balanced meal for yourself.

3. How do I know that I'm getting enough of everything I need? Do I need supplements?

This is covered in detail on pages 36-43 where Rosie has outlined the vitamins and minerals you need to be aware of, where to find them and whether there are any you need to supplement. The biggest take-home is that you just need a diverse diet: by eating a wide array of different ingredients you'll be able to look after yourself much better than eating the same few recipes day in, day out. In a nutshell: vitamin C, the B vitamins (bar B12), vitamin E, folate, potassium and magnesium are plentiful in a plant-based diet. It's important to be mindful of calcium, iron, zinc, iodine, selenium and omega-3 fatty acids, which are slightly less abundant, but nonetheless easy to get into the diet. The best sources of these are shared in Building a Balanced Plant-based Diet on pages 34–47. B12 and vitamin D need to be supplemented.

4. What are the best protein sources?

Not being able to get enough protein on a plant-based diet is a real myth. Almost no one in the Western world is deficient in protein and numerous studies show vegans consistently meet, if not surpass, the recommended daily allowance of protein, consuming 60–82g a day on average[1]. The NHS recommends 50g of protein per day and the most widely used reference point is 0.75 or 0.8 multiplied by each kilogram of body weight, so for someone who weighs 60kg that's 45–48g of protein each day.

Great plant-based sources of protein are: tofu, tempeh, edamame, peas, quinoa, all nuts/seeds/nut butters/tahini (including chia seeds, hemp seeds etc.), beans and legumes. Think about adding at least one source to each meal, e.g. porridge with hemp seeds and almond butter for breakfast, a roast veggie salad with lentils and a tahini dressing for lunch, and a tofu curry for dinner. It's really simple, but important to be mindful of.

5. Flexitarian versus plant-based: which is healthier?

Ultimately the benefits come from eating lots of fibre and fresh, wholefood ingredients instead of ultra-processed foods, which make up more than half of most people's diets. In my view, what you add to all that fresh food is up to you. If your diet is rooted in fruit, veg, beans, nuts, seeds and legumes, you'll likely feel much better.

6. Is a plant-based diet safe for both me and my family, smaller children and teenagers included?

It is. A range of professional organisations – including the NHS, British Dietetic Association, the Academy of Nutrition and Dietetics, the American Academy of Paediatrics, the Canadian Paediatric Society and Dietitians of Canada – all agree that appropriately planned vegetarian and vegan diets are not only safe but may provide certain health advantages. The important note here is 'appropriately planned'. Being truly aware of meeting your nutritional needs is essential in any diet, and it's really important in a plant-based diet. We'll go into all of the specific details of what that entails in Raising Plant-based Children on pages 48–61, so that you feel equipped and confident to make decisions both for yourself and your family.

7. Do you and your children eat the same meals?

Whenever we can. It doesn't always line up with work as getting out of the office on time is difficult, but it makes a world of difference to how much they eat and what they're willing to try when we do. During the UK's coronavirus lockdown we ate dinner together every night and it was heaven. Lots of the recipes in this book are based on those meals, recipes that are equally delicious for adults and children, because none of us have time to consistently make everyone separate meals. Our children certainly aren't perfect eaters, they have fussy periods and will absolutely say 'I don't like it' without even trying it, but the more we eat together the less stressful I find it (it also means that you're not going through the trouble of making a whole meal just for them, which they then refuse) and the more varied their diet is.

8. What are your thoughts on meat mimics?

I'm not a huge fan of meat replacements. I appreciate they may play a role in expanding the breadth of any diet that excludes meat, which at times is a brilliant thing. Likewise, what we eat every now and again will have little impact on our long-term wellbeing. That said, I do think we have to acknowledge them for what they are; they're almost exclusively ultra-processed with emulsifiers, additives and stabilizers. Increasing bodies of research show that these ingredients are detrimental to our health, and so shouldn't make up big parts of our diets. Emulsifiers, for example, can alter the bacteria in our gut (our microbiome) which can create chronic low-grade inflammation, with increasing links to metabolic disease, which refers to a cluster of diseases, including type 2 diabetes and obesity[2].

9. How do I get my partner to try it? They're very sceptical and it's holding me back.

This is a big barrier for so many people who want to change their diets. Sharing food is such a huge part of our culture and I found the idea of always eating something different very lonely, so I was really committed to finding a way to get my friends and family to try more plant-based food and drop the misconceptions that it was bland and restrictive. They were all completely new to the concept of a plant-based diet 10 years ago; no-one had tried a vegetarian diet, let alone a plant-based one. I knew they were sceptical and like so many, they worried it would be bland and unsatisfying. From day one I wanted to show that it wasn't, instead that it was abundant, colourful and rich in flavour. I let the food do the talking, I'd explain what was in the dish and how I'd cooked it, but never why it was healthy or imply that it was superior in any way. With some groups I'd also serve the plant-based option as the main initially, and some chicken, fish or cheese on the side, to make it feel more familiar, and that was highly effective in opening people's minds. Over time I dropped the sides, once they realised the plant-based option was more than enough in and of itself.

10. Socialising feels more challenging, any tips?

I definitely found this at the beginning – it can feel awkward doing something different to those around you. I have found it's become easier and easier, particularly over the last few years as plant-based options have become readily available and it's no longer a niche idea. I now find it genuinely easy to go to restaurants – there's always something good on the menu, but I understand if friends and family are cooking this can be trickier. What worked for me was cooking for them first, perhaps many times over, or offering to go and cook together, showing that eating plant-based food was both easy and delicious.

17

why the future needs to look different

why the future needs to look different

I've learnt so much over the last ten years. Ten years ago I had no understanding of the links between how we live and how we feel. As I started to join the dots and began to express those learnings, I saw a growing level of doubt and disbelief, and certainly dealt with an array of criticism from some people. Each year has, however, brought forward more evidence about the power our lifestyle has to inform our health. With that I've felt increasingly passionate about the need not to hide from the criticism but instead to take a stance on the conversation and do what I can to make the science easier to understand and more widely available – as I wish it had been for me when I was ill in 2011. At that time it felt as though I was wading through a minefield. So many of us have had the same experience, including **Dr Shireen Kassam**, who has reflected on the need to rectify that and bring lifestyle medicine to the forefront for us.

Shireen: lifestyle medicine

It took me 13 years as a practising doctor to realise there was more to medicine than pharmaceutical interventions, surgeries and technological solutions for established chronic conditions. Don't get me wrong, the field of medicine has seen some astonishing and ground-breaking advancements over the last century, but the focus of medical education, practice and research on a disease-oriented model of care has moved us away from understanding how to truly achieve optimal physical and mental health. A staggering 80% of chronic illness could be prevented or delayed through the adoption of healthy lifestyle habits[1].

Our move away from preventative medicine to a reactive healthcare model is disempowering and has led to a situation where we spend on average over a decade of our lives in ill health.

My journey into plant-based nutrition and lifestyle medicine began when I adopted a vegan diet for ethical reasons. I had been vegetarian since 2001, but by 2013 it was clear to me that consuming eggs and dairy was no longer aligned with my moral and ethical values. This change in diet sparked my interest in the science of plant-based nutrition and I was astounded to find an enormous wealth of evidence supporting a healthy vegan or plant-based diet for

A staggering 80% of chronic illness could be prevented or delayed through the adoption of healthy lifestyle habits.

Lifestyle medicine is the fastest-growing new medical speciality globally and strives to address the root cause of chronic illness by supporting and empowering individuals and communities to adopt healthy habits.

prevention, management and even reversal of chronic disease.

Through many hours of self-education and then formal qualifications a new way of practising medicine opened up to me. Lifestyle medicine[2] is the fastest-growing medical speciality globally and strives to address the root cause of chronic illness by supporting and empowering individuals and communities to adopt healthy habits, including a predominantly or exclusively plant-based diet. The success of lifestyle interventions has been so remarkable that more and more clinicians are adopting this way of practising medicine. To be able to heal chronic illness and support patients to thrive is one of the most rewarding aspects sof being a doctor.

Progress in incorporating plant-based nutrition into clinical practice is, however, slow and still considered a niche area. This is in part because the modern medical and healthcare curricula emphasise allopathic (medication and surgery) approaches over diet and lifestyle interventions. Educators and practitioners have not received adequate training in diet and lifestyle interventions and often assume

that patients will be unwilling to make the necessary changes to improve their health. Sadly, this means that most patients are not given the chance to take back control of their health and are left to explore diet and lifestyle options through mainstream media, which sometimes provides inaccurate and conflicting information.

In addition, our food environment is flooded with cheap, nutrient-deficient 'foods' that contribute to ill health rather than nourish us. The key players in the food industry are now so powerful that governments and policy makers have little influence over the provision of food to its citizens. This includes the animal agriculture industry that continues to influence dietary guidelines, public sector catering and food policy, perpetuating the myth that animal foods are essential in the diet. This could not be further from the truth. The only foods associated with good health and disease prevention are fruit, vegetables, whole grains, beans, nuts and seeds.

The narrative around plant-based nutrition and veganism more broadly is starting to shift as people increasingly realise that the food system is central to our most urgent global crises; health, climate and ecological. A transition to a just and sustainable food system is considered essential, without which we will continue to destroy nature, the planet and with it the health of humans and other animals. Adopting a plant-based diet is the single most impactful action you can take as an individual to improve the health of the planet. In addition, the health gains that will follow are huge with the possibility to vastly reduce the burden of chronic conditions. This includes significant reductions in the risk of heart disease, type 2 diabetes, obesity, dementia and certain cancers. The science is clear on this. What is good for the planet is good for personal and population health.

Bringing the medical community together

When I first started my education into plant-based nutrition, I realised that within the UK there was no structured or credible education programme. Most of my learning was coming from the USA, where the pioneers and early adopters of plant-based nutrition as a clinical intervention resided. So after five years of learning and assimilating I knew it was time to bring this education to the UK. I started by connecting a network of like-minded health professionals and forming a community interest company, Plant-Based Health Professionals UK (PBHP UK). We launched by holding the first medical conference on plant-based nutrition in medicine in March 2018. It was a sell-out event, and I knew there was a desire within the profession to learn more about this dietary approach and its profound impact on health. PBHP UK is a membership organisation open to everyone with a mission to provide evidence-based education on plant-based nutrition for the prevention of chronic illness. My approach has always been to infiltrate the conventional systems by providing education in a way that is relevant and consistent with our current medical approaches. We have also launched a regulated healthcare service, Plant Based Health Online, where people can access consultations with plant-based and lifestyle medicine doctors and practitioners who will support them to improve their health whilst minimising or eliminating the use of medications.

What a plant-based lifestyle means?

It's a philosophy and way of living that considers the health of humans, animals and the planet as equally important and intimately connected. To me, our disconnection from nature and each other is at the root of many of the problems we are facing.

Adopting a plant-based diet is the single most impactful action you can take as an individual to improve the health of the planet.

what is a healthy diet?

what is a healthy diet?

This is the question that I've asked myself countless times, as I'm sure you have too. I really struggled to get to grips with the extraordinary amount of information when I changed my diet in 2012, again something I'm sure lots of you can relate to. When I first began asking questions some doctors said lifestyle changes would have no effect, while a series of nutritionists and experts I came across recommended widely differing approaches to diet. There was so much opposing advice, what was important and what wasn't? Who should I listen to and who should I perhaps ignore? I felt it was almost impossible to understand at times. So, if that's where you are today, know you're not alone in the confusion and I hope that this section starts to unpick it for you.

I've asked **Dr Gemma Newman** and **Dr Alan Desmond**, both NHS doctors, to spell it all out, to help us get to the bottom of what a healthy diet really is.

Gemma: a healthy diet

No doubt you have noticed countless magazine articles, diet books and TV shows over the decades talking about how to get the perfect body, lose that excess weight or get your dream six-pack. The 'ideal' body shape has varied throughout the decades, but the pressure to look a certain way remains. From 'cut the carbs' to 'keto cures all' and everything in between, the advice we see can be conflicting to say the least. Meanwhile, healthy messages around food are lacking; how rarely do you see articles with useful headlines such as 'what is the optimal diet to prevent cancer?', 'how to fuel your body to slash the risk of heart disease?' or 'what foods could reduce the risk of asthma for your child?', rather than ones that focus on getting that 'bikini-ready body'? And then when you start a family, there is even more pressure; not only to look a certain way but to raise your children 'the right way'. What milk should you should give your baby? Which sleep training technique is best? Finger foods or purées? Are they eating enough fruit and veg? I could go on! For so many families, there are also barriers to healthy options. For busy parents working full time to make ends meet, cheap packaged foods with a long shelf life become the logical choice. Time, finances and the mental bandwidth to cook a meal are very often in short supply, coupled with an overwhelming amount of advice, judgement and confusion, for all of us, at every stage of life. Diet culture and our natural desire for a quick fix also make it really appealing to try the latest fad. On top of that, scary headlines about both adults and children not getting the right nutrients on a plant-based diet make the question of how to feed yourself and your family a plant-based diet far more confusing than it needs to be.

The truth is a healthy diet is about how we feel day to day – not how we look – and crucially, it's about living a life that reduces the risk of our biggest killers. It's also far simpler than many of us think. Research shows the best way to achieve a healthy diet for you and for your family is through simple shifts towards healthy choices that you can keep doing indefinitely, and that feel easy and manageable. Adding in more of the foods that will nourish and sustain you, whilst making the foods that provide empty calories or that are classed as 'ultra-processed' less of a staple.

Can my diet change my health?

According to the World Health Organization[1], 71% of all deaths around the world each year – a whopping 41 million people – are caused by diseases linked to our lifestyles (the scientific word for these are 'non-communicable diseases', or non-infectious health conditions). Just four health conditions – heart disease, cancers, lung disease and diabetes – account for 80% of premature deaths. And incredibly, about 80% of these premature deaths could be prevented by adopting four healthy lifestyle factors; a healthy diet, regular physical activity, not smoking and sensible use of alcohol[2]. Does this surprise you? Perhaps you are wondering why you had never heard this before? As a doctor, most of what I deal with day to day is helping people through when they are already affected by these conditions – how wonderful it is to be able to share this information with you and your family *before* they begin to live with a life limiting disease.

Is there one healthy habit that has the highest impact? The answer seems to be the food we put on our plates. Globally, it is reported that unhealthy diets contribute to more death and disability than smoking, alcohol and drug use combined. The most comprehensive analysis of dietary risk factors has determined that around the world, one in five deaths are caused by an unhealthy diet[3]. The top five indicators of an unhealthy diet were high salt intakes (mainly a reflection of eating ultra-processed foods), and low intakes of whole grains, fruit, nuts/seeds and vegetables.

A study using data from the Nurses' Health Study and the Health Professionals Follow-up Study in the USA, involving more than 170,000 men and women, defined a few crucial healthy habits: a healthy diet; maintaining a normal body mass index (BMI); never smoking; avoiding excess alcohol and enjoying more than 30 minutes of moderate to high energy activity per day[4]. During the 34 years of follow-up, with each healthy habit there was a significant reduction in the chance of living with a chronic disease, *and* a reduction in the total risk of death. Sticking to all four of the healthy factors meant you were 65% less likely to die of cancer and 82% less likely to die of heart disease. And it's never too late; sticking to these healthy habits lengthened life from the age of 50 by a massive 14 years in women and 12 years in men. In this study, a healthy diet was defined as one that was high in whole plant foods including fruits, vegetables, unsaturated fats, omega-3 fatty acids and whole grains, and an eating pattern low in processed meat, red meat, processed food, salt and sugar sweetened drinks.

The data is clear: eating more plants and more fresh food is a huge part of yours and your family's health solution.

Data from the UK showed similar results[5.] The study involving 4,886 men and women defined four unhealthy habits; smoking, low fruit and vegetable consumption, minimal physical activity and high alcohol consumption. With an average follow up of 20 years, each unhealthy habit contributed to a significantly increased risk of dying from any cause, and those with all four had a 12-year reduction in life expectancy. The data is clear: eating more plants and more fresh food is a huge part of yours and your family's health solution.

Do I need to go fully plant-based?

I get asked this question a lot, and the short answer is no. There is more than one way to eat healthily, just as there is more than one way to eat unhealthily. You must decide what feels right for you. Most importantly, you – and only you – can decide what it is you feel you can include and maintain as a habit in your life, rather than a 'quick-fix'. But by increasing your intake of plant-based wholefoods, the evidence shows you can only do good for your health long-term.

Fruit and vegetables are full of antioxidants, vitamins, minerals, fibre and phytochemicals. By eating nature's 'rainbow' and looking to include as many different colours of plant foods as possible, you'll find the best way to ensure you are eating a wide variety of these phytochemicals. Phytochemicals are naturally occurring chemicals produced by plants, and they function to protect plants (against invasion, the sun's rays, disease, and infection) but they also can do us a lot of good too. Evidence shows that taking phytochemicals in supplement form does not provide the same benefits.

Fruit and vegetables, along with wholegrains and beans, are also our only sources of dietary fibre too, which plays an important role in our health and the maintenance of a healthy microbiome. Other health benefits? By loading up on anti-inflammatory foods with plenty of colourful fruit and vegetables, we are giving our bodies a powerful weapon to fight inflammation. If free radicals in the body are like small fires, creating the inflammation, imagine the antioxidants in fruit and vegetables as tiny fire engines putting them out. Reducing oxidative stress in the body also helps to slow the ageing process at a cellular level, and in fact some of the longest living populations in the world enjoy a 95% plant-based diet. These areas of the world were defined as the 'Blue Zones®' by National Geographic researcher Dan Buettner. In these places – Okinawa (Japan); Sardinia (Italy); Nicoya (Costa Rica); Icaria (Greece) and among the Seventh-day Adventists in Loma Linda (California) – the people tend to be very healthy and active into their eighties and nineties, and they have much lower rates of chronic disease. So, they not only live longer but they also live better. Food wise, the cuisine in each place was very different, but there were parallels among the core ingredients. The foods they had in common were nuts and seeds, healthy wholegrains, and lots of vegetables alongside a cup of beans, or pulses per day. The Blue Zones® also share important lifestyle similarities, such as making movement throughout the day a natural way of life, having purpose in their lives, having strong family links, and incorporating stress-relieving habits into their day. As you can see, it's not all about the food, but whole plant foods are one of the fundamental backbones of the daily habits that help these populations stay healthy for so long.

The power of plants

We have touched on some of the reasons why wholefood plant-based lifestyles can be helpful to us in minimising inflammation, oxidative stress and the ageing process, as well as maximising fibre, vitamins, minerals and phytochemicals, all of which improve our overall health. Research has shown us that there are also several specific health concerns that can also be improved through a daily habit of eating more plants too. By increasing our intake of plants, we can:

- Reduce the risk of developing the vast majority of heart disease.
- Reduce the risk of developing most cancers.
- Prevent us from developing type 2 diabetes and help us reverse it.
- Improve our mental health.
- Maintain a healthy gut, eliminate diverticular disease and certain forms of IBS.
- Improve our hormone regulation and keep the thyroid healthy.
- Support immunity.

It may seem too good to be true, and certainly a healthy plant-focussed diet is not the panacea it is sometimes made out to be. Many of us will still experience chronic disease, despite a healthy lifestyle. There is no magic pill, or cure all. But the data does speak to the above and I have seen some incredible transformations in my own family and in the lives of my patients. From elderly patients with improvements in arthritis and blood pressure readings, to regression of prostate cancer, elimination of Crohn's disease, improved endometriosis and psoriasis to name just a few. Often, these patients also found unintended side effects of their lifestyle changes; one woman was hoping to improve her asthma but found that her chronic kidney disease also improved. One woman who was hoping to improve her menopausal symptoms noticed a dramatic improvement to her mood and her lupus. We are not simply the

diseases we experience; we are whole beings. Sometimes holistic approaches to health also produce holistic results in other aspects of our lives which are truly wonderful to see.

The six components of lifestyle medicine are good nutrition, exercise, avoidance of tobacco, exercise, sleep, stress management and healthy relationships. When it comes to food, the founding organisation of the global lifestyle medicine movement – The American College of Lifestyle Medicine – defines the optimal diet as 'an eating plan based predominantly on a variety of minimally processed vegetables, fruits, whole grains, legumes, nuts and seeds'. This is the essence of a whole food plant-based diet. Hopefully you are ready to dive in and give it a try – for your own health and for your loved ones too.

As Gemma said, really healthy eating is simple: more broccoli, more chickpeas, more spinach, less foods with ingredients that we can't pronounce. As we've touched on, these are loaded with fibre, which is essential to promoting good gut health, which, as **Dr Alan Desmond**, consultant gastroenterologist, explains, is a vital consideration as part of a healthy diet.

Alan: health begins in the gut

As a doctor who specialises in gut health problems, my patients ask me about food all the time. Throughout my career, I have been determined to provide evidence-based answers to that all-important question: 'what should I eat?' Having spent years immersed in the research on food and digestive heath I am convinced that the best advice is to avoid eating processed foods and to replace animal products with healthier, plant-based sources of nutrients. An approach to food that embraces a variety of fruits, vegetables,

29

whole grains, beans, legumes, nuts and seeds. The logical conclusion? A whole-food, plant-based diet. I now start conversations with my patients by asking about the foods they eat each day. Evidence-based dietary advice helps my patients to get the best possible outcomes. The health transformations I have seen at my clinic have inspired me to share the evidence on food and gut health with as many people as possible. I'm very happy to be sharing it with you.

The concept that digestive health influences our overall wellbeing is not new. Over two thousand years ago the so-called father of modern medicine, Hippocrates, taught his students that 'all disease begins in the gut'. In the last 20 years, new insights into the importance of our gut's immune system, the role of our gut health in our overall wellbeing and the composition of the gut microbiome, have revealed that there is a lot of truth in this ancient wisdom.

Gut health 101

Before we go further, I wanted to explain what the gut microbiome is and why it matters. Each one of us carries up to 100 trillion microbes in our gut. These microscopic bacteria, viruses, yeasts and archaea, make up our gut 'microbiome', which contains just as many cells and 100 times more genetic material than the rest of our body combined. Throughout our lives, these bugs help us to digest our food, control our blood sugars, maintain a healthy weight, and even help to improve our mood. They can also protect us from numerous digestive conditions including Crohn's disease, colitis and bowel cancer.

Our personal microbiome begins to form at birth. With our first breath and our first human touch, our microbial population begins to take shape. It gets to work quickly, helping us to digest our

first meal. Our mother's milk doesn't just provide calories, it also contains live beneficial bacteria (probiotics) and substances to promote the growth of our own healthy bacteria (prebiotics).

The gut microbiome has recently been recognised as 'a control centre for human biology'. This is a crucially important concept, as we can choose to support our gut microbial health through our food choices and lifestyle. As you pick the ingredients for your next meal, you might like to consider the following question: 'What kind of gut microbiome am I building today?'

Plant-based versus omnivore

As adults, the foods we eat each day are the main determinant of our gut microbial health. The Standard Western Diet promotes a microbiome that thrives on animal protein – also known as a 'proteolytic gut microbiome'. This type of microbiome produces biologically active substances, including ammonia, indolic and phenolic compounds, branch-chain amino acids and trimethylamine. These are harmful metabolites known to increase our risks of cardiovascular disease, type 2 diabetes and other chronic medical conditions.

In fact, most of the products generated by this Standard Western Diet microbiome are considered detrimental to overall health and wellbeing. In contrast, when you choose to eat meals built around fruits, vegetables, whole grains, beans, nuts and seeds, you are choosing to build a gut microbiome that becomes optimised for the production of substances called 'short-chain fatty-acids' or SCFAs. The health effects of SCFAs are astounding. They combat chronic inflammation, help to control our appetite, keep our blood sugar level, and even provide nourishment to the cells lining our gut. A plant-fuelled microbiome does its best to keep its human host as healthy as possible!

Junk foods versus gut health

The healthiest version of a plant-based diet is built from 'whole foods'. In industrialised countries like the US and the UK, highly processed products like biscuits, mass-produced buns and breads, meat pies, sausage rolls, artificial ice creams, flavoured yoghurts and sweetened fizzy drinks now make up over half of all calories consumed. These so-called 'junk foods' are shelf-stable, easy to store, and may even taste nice, but the artificial fillers, flavour enhancers, emulsifiers and stabilisers for chemicals they contain have no business in the human digestive system.

Covering an area about the size of a large garden, our gut barrier is our gut's first line of defence. It works hard to keep potentially harmful bugs and other substances from entering our bloodstream.

Chemicals present in highly processed foods, such as maltodextrin (an additive), polysorbate-80 (a common emulsifier) and carboxymethylcellulose (another emulsifier) launch a two-pronged attack on the integrity of this barrier: promoting the growth of harmful gut bacteria while actively degrading our gut's delicate defense mechanisms. This allows harmful bacteria and their by-products to breach our defences, come into direct contact with our immune system and trigger abnormal inflammatory responses in our gut and around our body. 'Ditch the junk-foods' is one of the key pieces of advice that I give to my patients with gut health issues. It's one change we can all make to protect our digestive health.

The gut–immune connection

Our gut microbial health and our immune health depend upon each other. Although most people don't immediately associate the gut with their immune system, we now understand that more than 60% of our body's immune cells lie within the digestive tract. Our gut microbes help to educate our immune system and help prevent the immune over-activity that contributes to conditions like type 1 diabetes, rheumatoid arthritis, coeliac disease and allergies. Fibre-filled meals allow our gut microbes to maximise their production of 'short-chain fatty acids' – substances that helps our immune system to function efficiently, fighting infections and even identifying and eliminating early cancerous cells.

The importance of our immune health has really been emphasised during the COVID-19 pandemic. In 2020 researchers described for the first time how an unhealthy gut microbiome – with reduced levels of the bacteria that thrive in a high-fibre environment – predicted higher levels of lung inflammation in patients hospitalised with this new disease. Further studies showed that during the first wave of the pandemic, front-line doctors who described their diet as 'vegan or whole-food or plant-based', were far less likely to become gravely ill when they caught COVID-19. Research has also shown that people with the highest intake of plants in their diet are 40% less likely to have a severe disease course. When it comes to protecting our immune health, food really does matter.

Fermented foods: nature's microbiome boost

Plant-based fermented foods have been around since the dawn of human civilisation. The ancient techniques used to produce them take advantage of the ability of bacterial cultures to break down and ferment foods, radically changing their taste and flavour profile. Fermented foods, such as tempeh, miso, sauerkraut and kimchi can contain dozens or even hundreds of bacterial strains. Most fermented foods have a predominance of lactic acid bacteria, the kind of bacteria that promotes a healthier gut microbiome.

Numerous studies have suggested that fermented foods may have unique health benefits. For example, eating a daily serving of kimchi improved glucose control and improved insulin sensitivity in volunteers with pre-diabetes. Other researchers have suggested that fermented soy products – like natto, miso and tempeh – can help to reduce body fat and improve cholesterol. In 2021, researchers at Stanford University showed that a diet high in fermented foods, including kimchi, fermented vegetables, vegetable brine drinks and kombucha tea can result in unique gut health benefits. In just 10 weeks, their volunteers achieved significant increases in gut microbial diversity, with simultaneous reductions in pro-inflammatory proteins.

I enjoy fermented foods as a tasty and interesting addition to my plant-based diet, with some bonus benefits for my gut microbiome. If you don't enjoy them, don't worry. Kimchi and sauerkraut aren't yet considered essential foods. Besides which, eating raw fruits and vegetables naturally provides the very same beneficial bacteria that are found in fermented foods.

How to beat the gas and learn to love legumes!

Legumes – beans, peas, lentils, and split peas – are a crucial part of a healthy diet. Many of their benefits are derived from their ability to promote fermentation and a healthier gut microbiome. This natural and beneficial process also produces digestive gas. Gas in your gut – and leaving your gut – is a normal and healthy part of digestion. For some people, introducing legumes for the first time can bring on a degree of bloating and discomfort. In my experience, the digestive issues that sometimes accompany an increase in bean consumption tends to settle within a few weeks. Here are some practical tips to help you and your gut along the way.

1. Try tofu, tempeh and hummus: these foods are all made from legumes but produce less fermentation and less gas.

2. Start slow: try eating just a tablespoon of beans a day for a few weeks, then ramp up the quantity slowly, giving your GI tract and microbiome time to adjust.

3. Digestive enzymes: adding a few capsules of galactosidase digestive enzyme before a legume-rich meal can be a gamechanger. There are many inexpensive brands available.

4. Soak and rinse: soaking your dried beans overnight, and rinsing before cooking helps reduce the fermentation.

5. Cook well: make sure your legumes are well done. Better still, buy precooked and ready-to-eat legumes in tins or jars. The high temperatures used in commercial kitchens break down the fermentable carbohydrates, so you will experience less bloating.

6. And finally, take a bean break: spend a few months focusing on the overall healthfulness of your diet, sleep and exercise. Then come back to try legumes when you feel ready.

Build a healthier gut microbiome

The more we learn about the benefits of a healthy gut microbiome, the more apparent it becomes that our gut microbes want to keep us (their human hosts) as healthy as possible, for as long as possible. Here are several practices that you can use to support your gut microbial health each day.

1. Eat a variety of plants. Our healthy bacteria absolutely love plant fibre. This was confirmed when the American Gut Project analysed the gut microbiomes of over 11,000 volunteers from around the world. Their huge scientific effort showed that the key to maintaining a healthy and diverse microbiome is to eat lots of plants and to eat a variety. Every plant-based food, be it a bean, green or whole grain, contains different types of fibre and important phytonutrients. Our microbiome loves them all. Aiming for more than 30 different plants per week is a great initial target. Once you've made the switch to a plant-based diet you will easily exceed this number and achieve a level of plant-diversity rarely seen in industrialised countries!

2. Get enough sleep. The bugs of our microbiome seem to work on the same 24-hour daily cycle as the rest of our body. In fact, some researchers believe that our microbiome plays an important role in setting our body clock. Sleep deprivation, jet lag and shift work have all been linked to reduced microbial diversity. Show your microbiome some love by getting seven to eight hours of restful sleep.

3. Make exercise part of your routine. In 2014, a team of Irish researchers found that elite rugby players displayed an impressive level of microbiome diversity. Further studies have shown that we can all reap the gut-health benefits of regular exercise, which helps to boost levels of healthy, fibre-loving bacteria.

4. Spend time in nature. A sanitised indoor lifestyle is not the best thing for our microbial health. We know that people who live in the countryside tend to have healthier, more diverse microbiomes than city dwellers. If you can't make it to the great outdoors, even spending time in parks or gardens can be beneficial.

5. Avoid unnecessary antibiotics. Antibiotics have been of incredible benefit to humankind, helping us fight common serious infections such as pneumonia and meningitis. However, if you have a simple cough or cold that your doctor feels will settle without antibiotics, then do your microbiome a favour and take their advice. A single course of antibiotics can dramatically alter the balance and diversity of the human microbiome. If you do need antibiotic treatment, then you can help your gut bugs to recover by leaning into the practices above. Another way to avoid excess antibiotics is to remove meat and dairy from your diet. Most of the antibiotics used in the world are given to farmed animals. These antibiotics remain in the food chain and may negatively affect the human microbiome.

It's no coincidence that these tips for a healthy microbiome sound a lot like Ella's advice for overall health and happiness. A plant-based diet, exercise, adequate sleep and spending time in nature are common practices among the inhabitants of the Blue Zones®; the areas of the world where people live the longest and healthiest lives. Our health and happiness may well depend upon on our gut microbiome. Being kind to our gut bugs means being kind to ourselves!

building a balanced plant-based diet

building a balanced plant-based diet

We know the power of a plant-based diet, and of course this book is filled with over a hundred recipes to get you started or support you in continuing on your journey. I really want to help you go beyond that though, so that your time in the kitchen becomes much more than just following a recipe. I want to ensure you feel comfortable and confident putting meals together yourself knowing that you're meeting your nutritional needs. Of course, not every meal is going to include every nutrient and meet every requirement – that would make eating in restaurants, for example, extraordinarily reductive. Food also has to be fun. We're not looking for 'perfect' every time, but to expand our knowledge so that we have an awareness of the importance of eating foods that contain omega-3s or which are the nutritious sources of plant protein, for example. In doing that we can mindfully check off those needs across the week. To help us do that, **Rosie Martin**, a registered dietician who specialises in helping her clients transition to a healthy, balanced, plant-based diet has put together an incredibly comprehensive guide.

Rosie: my experience of a plant-based diet

Through my practice, I regularly support people in their transition to a plant-based lifestyle. Aside from the planetary and animal welfare advantages, the long list of health benefits reported by my clients continues to grow. Many people find that they have more energy, feel lighter after meals, recover more quickly from exercise, sleep better and can manage their weight more easily. Although these accounts are anecdotal, a growing body of evidence is clarifying the science behind these experiences.

I have coeliac disease, a condition that causes inflammation and damage to my small intestine if I eat gluten. Despite following a gluten-free diet since my first year of life, I experienced digestive issues for much of my childhood and teenage years. It was only when I moved to a plant-based diet, and therefore increased the fibre and diversity of plant foods I ate, that I understood what a healthy digestive system feels like, and it changed my life! Through this transition, I discovered a passion for food and creating innovative and delicious meals exclusively using plant foods. In addition, my new-found appetite for nutrition science lead me on my path to becoming a registered dietician and enabled me to support others in embracing the power of plants.

Before we get into the detail, I wanted to show you a visual guide to a balanced diet. The good news is that with a little knowledge, building a healthy plant-based diet becomes simple. If you're able to regularly build your plate based on the principles opposite, you'll get everything you need. Of course, it doesn't have to be followed exactly at every meal, not everything we choose to make or

what a balanced plate looks like

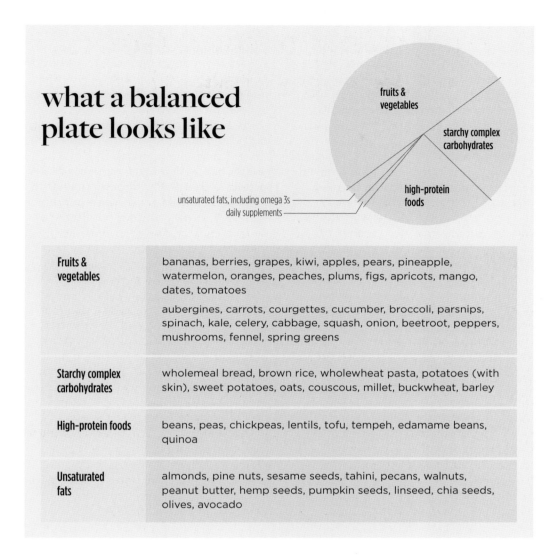

Fruits & vegetables	bananas, berries, grapes, kiwi, apples, pears, pineapple, watermelon, oranges, peaches, plums, figs, apricots, mango, dates, tomatoes
	aubergines, carrots, courgettes, cucumber, broccoli, parsnips, spinach, kale, celery, cabbage, squash, onion, beetroot, peppers, mushrooms, fennel, spring greens
Starchy complex carbohydrates	wholemeal bread, brown rice, wholewheat pasta, potatoes (with skin), sweet potatoes, oats, couscous, millet, buckwheat, barley
High-protein foods	beans, peas, chickpeas, lentils, tofu, tempeh, edamame beans, quinoa
Unsaturated fats	almonds, pine nuts, sesame seeds, tahini, pecans, walnuts, peanut butter, hemp seeds, pumpkin seeds, linseed, chia seeds, olives, avocado

consume will meet these exact criteria and it's incredibly important not to get too hung up on an idea of 'perfection' – food is also for enjoyment – but you can use this as a general guide for your overall dietary pattern. The main thing to note is to try and include a variety of different and colourful plant foods in your diet. This will maximise the range of micronutrients, fibre and other beneficial plant compounds, including antioxidants and phytonutrients which, as Gemma explained earlier, have hugely positive effects on our health.

As we get a little more into the detail, into why these foods matter and where to find them, I want to start with the macronutrients – carbohydrates, proteins and fats – these make up the bulk of our diet.

Macronutrients

These essential components of our food make up the fuel we need to live, providing us with energy and raw materials for cell structure and function. Day and night, we use energy from macronutrients for everything, from

37

breathing and keeping our heart beating to digesting our food, regulating our body temperature and regenerating the cells of our body. To put it really simply, we want a balance of complex carbohydrates, proteins and healthy fats in our meals to keep our bodies going.

Carbohydrates
Carbohydrates are our body's preferred source of energy and should make up around 45–65% of our total energy intake through the day. When we eat carbohydrates, our digestive system breaks them down into sugars. Our body absorbs these sugars and releases them as energy to power life-giving processes, such as movement and brain function. Carbohydrates also provide the building blocks required to make hormones such as serotonin, the hormone that makes us feel happy. In addition, carbohydrates provide fibre, which supports the health-promoting bacteria that live in our gut.

sources of nutrients

Zinc	oats, chickpeas, walnuts, hemp seeds, pumpkin seeds, cashews, quinoa, lentils, tofu, brown and wild rice, black beans, pecans, peas, wholemeal bread, tempeh and fortified nutritional yeast
Calcium	tofu, tempeh, chickpeas, haricot beans, canellini beans, butter beans, black beans, kidney beans, almonds, Brazil nuts, tahini, chia seeds, linseed, kale, watercress, broccoli, figs, oranges, fortified plant milks
Iron	tofu, tempeh, edamame, chickpeas, lentils, black beans, kidney beans, canellini beans, butter beans, pumpkin seeds, tahini, sunflower seeds, oats, chia seeds, almonds, cashews, kale, potatoes (with skin on), quinoa, wholewheat pasta, spinach
Selenium	Brazil nuts, other sources, but in small amounts: brown rice, quinoa, sunflower seeds, mushrooms, oats, spinach, lentils, cashews
Iodine	iodised salt, iodine fortified plant milks, occasional seaweed
Omega 3	walnuts (6 halves daily), linseed, hemp and chia seeds (2 tablespoons daily)
Daily supplements	vitamin B12: at least 10µg daily, 2000µg weekly, or consume B12-fortified foods twice daily vitamin D: 10µg daily iodine: 150µcg daily from non-seaweed supplements or fortified foods selenium: 60–75µg or consume 2 Brazil nuts daily omega-3 (optional): algae oil containing around 450mg combined EPA and DHA

Most of us aren't getting anywhere near enough fibre and it's so important. We should be aiming for 30g a day. That could look like porridge with berries and chopped nuts for breakfast, a quinoa salad with veggies and hummus for lunch, an apple with peanut butter in the afternoon, and a red lentil dhal with brown rice for dinner. Across each week we should aim to eat 30 different plant-based foods to support our gut health.

While carbohydrates are essential, the type we eat makes a big difference to our energy levels and wellbeing. We can simplify this by putting carbohydrates into two categories:

Complex carbohydrates are found in fruits, vegetables, beans and whole grains (see page 37 for examples). These carbohydrates are full of beneficial fibre, antioxidants, vitamins and minerals. They help keep us full and provide us with sustained energy levels through the day.

Simple carbohydrates are found in sugars, white flour and fizzy drinks. Many of these carbohydrates are highly processed and have been stripped of the beneficial components found in complex carbohydrates, including fibre. Generally they're not considered advantageous for health, in part because they can be broken down much more quickly by the body, causing blood sugar spikes and then crashes, which in turn lead to lethargy and food cravings, and so they won't keep us energised across the day.

Protein

Protein is another vital nutrient and is found in every cell of the human body. It is involved in all processes in the body, from energy production, supporting the transportation of substances (vitamins, minerals, oxygen) and speeding up chemical reactions by creating molecules called enzymes, to building hormones and neurotransmitters (which affect our mood and emotions) and allowing our hormones and immune system to work effectively. It's also essential for building and repairing cells and tissue, including the skin, hair, muscle and bone.

Healthy adults require approximately 0.75–0.8g of protein per kilogram of body weight each day. For example, if you weighed 60kg your daily protein needs would be roughly 45-48g. If you are an athlete or you have any medical issues, your requirements for protein may go up.

Protein is made up of 20 different amino acids, or 'building blocks', which can be reconfigured to create thousands of different cells and molecules to form our tissues and organs. Nine of the twenty amino acids are termed 'essential', meaning that our bodies cannot make them and we therefore need to consume them as part of our diet.

There is a common concern when moving towards a plant-based diet that getting enough protein will be difficult. That isn't the case, however. For a healthy person on a varied diet, filling a quarter of your plate with protein-rich plant foods (see page 37), will cover your protein requirements.

For example, enjoying your porridge with 2 tablespoons of hemp seeds, 1 tablespoon almond butter and 200ml of soya milk in the morning; adding 100g of hummus and a 30g sprinkle of pumpkin seeds to your lunch and finishing the day with a stir fry using 100g of tofu and a handful of edamame beans will take you over 50g of protein.

There's also a concern that you can't get all the essential amino acids you need on a plant-based diet. Again, rest assured that all nine essential amino acids can be found in varying quantities in plant food, so you don't need to consume animal-based foods to get adequate protein. It's helpful to understand where that concern comes from though. Animal proteins contain good quantities of all nine essential amino acids, which is why you may have heard animal protein referred to as 'complete'. Plant proteins tend to have less of one amino acid, and so have been referred to as 'incomplete'. This is nothing to worry about though, as plant proteins are not all low in the same amino acids. Beans, for example, are typically lower in an amino acid called methionine, which is plentiful in grains. So, if you had nut butter on whole grain toast, toasted seeds in a lentil salad or hummus with brown rice and veggies your meal would be 'complete'.

Simply put, if you're eating a mix of beans, whole grains, nuts, seeds and soy products in your diet you'll have no problem getting all the amino acids you need. Really it just continues to highlight the importance of eating a wide variety of foods across the day.

Fat

Fat is vital for our health. It's an important source of energy and plays an essential role in brain function, hormone production, protecting vital organs and the absorption of vitamins. Fat comes in two main forms: saturated and unsaturated. Saturated fats are derived predominantly from animal-based foods. We should be keeping our intake of saturated fat low, as it is linked to a rise in levels of low-density lipoprotein cholesterol (LDL-C) in our blood. LDL-C is considered an unhealthy form of cholesterol as it has been directly linked to narrowing of blood vessels through the process of atherosclerosis,

increasing our risk of heart disease. The NHS recommends no more than 30g a day for men and 20g for women. Likewise, the UK's Scientific Advisory Committee on Nutrition (SACN) and the Dietary Guidelines for Americans recommend limiting saturated fat to 10% or fewer of your daily calories.

On a plant-based diet the main sources of saturated fats are coconut oil and cacao fat. These are absolutely fine to include in a healthy diet, but not in every meal, every day. Although some research suggests that not all saturated fats are equal, we know that switching them for unsaturated fats is a positive choice for cardiovascular health.

When we move towards a diet that is based on more whole plants, we tend to reduce our intake of saturated fat and increase the beneficial unsaturated fats (polyunsaturated and monounsaturated) from plants like avocado, olives, nuts and seeds.

Trans fatty acids, or trans fats, are a type of fat that raise LDL-C much like saturated fats. In addition, trans fats have also been shown to lower high-density lipoprotein cholesterol (HDL-C), which is known as the healthy form of cholesterol. Trans fats provide no nutritional value and are detrimental to heart health. Due to these health concerns, manufacturers have lowered the levels of trans fats in their packaged foods, but trans fats can still be found in ready-made cakes, biscuits, margarines, takeaways, pastries and fried foods. They won't always be listed as 'trans fats' on food labels, so watch out for 'hydrogenated fats' or 'partially hydrogenated vegetable oils'.

Omega-3 fatty acids

These are essential dietary fats, which are important for our brain and immune health, as well as playing an anti-inflammatory role in the body. The three important omega-3 fatty acids to be aware of are alpha-linolenic acid (ALA), eicosapentaenoic acid (EPA), and docosahexaenoic acid (DHA). On a plant-based diet you can get your ALA by eating two tablespoons of linseed (also known as flaxseed), hemp or chia seeds, or six walnut halves each day.

EPA and DHA, on the other hand, cannot be obtained directly on a plant-based diet, as our main source is oily fish. Our bodies can convert the ALA we eat into EPA and DHA, though unfortunately, the rate of conversion can be poor, so many people choose to supplement. Algae, a small, plant-like organism found in the ocean, provides a rich source of EPA and DHA; in fact this is where the fish originally get theirs. If you are on a plant-based diet, you can avoid the fish and go straight to the source by taking an algae oil supplement, aiming for around 450mg of combined EPA and DHA per day. It's shown to be as bio-available (easily absorbed) in the body as salmon, so by taking it this way you don't need to worry about not having enough omega-3.

Micronutrients

Unlike the macronutrients, which we need in large quantities for fuel, we need smaller quantities of micronutrients – vitamins and minerals. They are, however, absolutely vital for energy levels, bone health, growth, an optimum immune system and reducing our risk of disease.

A plant-based diet is rich in many of the vitamins and minerals we need. Vitamin E is found in avocados, spinach, nuts, seeds and sunflower oil and acts as an antioxidant, protecting cells from damage. Vitamin C is also an antioxidant found in many fruits and vegetables including blackberries, strawberries,

kiwis, peas, broccoli and peppers. Vitamin C protects cells, promotes wound healing and maintains healthy tissues, like our skin, bones and collagen. Folate is found in avocados, broccoli, spinach, beans and peanuts, and is required to form our DNA and support cell division. Potassium is a mineral that supports heart function and it can be found in many plant foods, including bananas, dates, parsnips, swiss chard, beet greens, black beans and almonds. Magnesium is important for bone health and metabolism and is abundant in spinach, tahini, almonds and tofu.

There are a few micronutrients that we do need to be mindful of when planning a healthy plant-based diet; they are readily available but we need to ensure we're eating enough of them.

Calcium

Calcium is a key mineral for bone health, muscle movement and blood clotting. For great sources of calcium turn to page 38. An example day to reach your calcium requirements of 700mg could look like: 200ml of fortified plant milk in your porridge or smoothie in the morning and a 100g portion of tofu and 70g kale in either your lunch or dinner.

Iron

Iron is required for the body to grow and develop. It is also used to make a vital protein called haemoglobin that transports oxygen around the body via our blood vessels. Recommendations for men are 8.7mg per day, whereas for women they are higher, at 14.8mg per day. Iron deficiency is common across all dietary patterns therefore everyone should ensure they consume adequate amounts. For good plant-based sources turn to page 38. You can boost your absorption of iron from plants dramatically by consuming iron-rich foods alongside a source of vitamin

C, such as broccoli, peppers, kiwis or strawberries and avoiding drinking tea or coffee with meals.

To reach the daily iron requirement of 14.8mg an example day could look like: 2 tablespoons of pumpkin seeds and a handful of cashew nuts with breakfast; 100g quinoa drizzled with 2 teaspoons tahini with lunch, and wholewheat pasta with the evening meal.

Selenium

Selenium is another antioxidant that helps us to achieve healthy hair and nails, a well-functioning immune system, and normal sperm production in men. It is found in small amounts in a variety of whole plant foods including brown rice and lentils, but an easy way to meet your daily dose is to eat two Brazil nuts.

Zinc

We require zinc for healthy hair and nails, but it also supports our DNA, fertility and brain function. Zinc is found in many whole plant foods (see the list on page 38). Include these healthy foods regularly to meet your zinc requirements. Zinc absorption can be increased by eating fermented soya products (such as miso and tempeh), soaking and rinsing dried beans before cooking, and sprouting grains and seeds before consuming. To reach the daily zinc requirements of 7mg for women and 9.5mg for men an example day could look like: a handful of cashew nuts with breakfast, 2 tablespoons of sunflower seeds sprinkled on a salad or as a snack, and 1 tablespoon of fortified nutritional yeast with an evening meal.

Supplements

Although supplementing may seem 'unnatural', our modern lifestyles, changes in how we produce food, and our increasing understanding of nutrition, means that much of the population already relies on food fortification and added supplements. For example, many basic staple foods such as white flour, cereals and milk are fortified with nutrients such as calcium, iron and vitamin D in the UK. Although it is preferable to get nutrients from food, there are some that are more difficult to get on a fully plant-based diet and so it is wise to supplement. This is what is recommended as daily supplementation:

Vitamin B12

Vitamin B12 is crucial for our nervous system and blood cells. As the only vitamin that cannot be obtained from plants because it is created by bacteria, everyone on a long-term plant-based diet should supplement with at least 10µg of vitamin B12 daily, or 2000µg weekly. Alternatively you can include foods with added B12 at least twice every day. These could include fortified plant-based milks, nutritional yeast flakes or yeast extracts.

Vitamin D

Vitamin D is required to maintain bone strength. Regardless of your dietary pattern, everyone should consider taking a daily vitamin D supplement of 10µg. This is particularly important through the winter months, as our main source is from production in our skin on exposure to summer sunlight.

Iodine

We need iodine for thyroid function and to support our metabolism. Most people get iodine from dairy products through supplemented cattle feed. Seaweed is a concentrated source of iodine, but due to the huge variations in iodine content, and the health consequences of having too much or too little, we can't generally rely on seaweed for our daily dose. Some plant milks and salts are fortified with a non-seaweed source of iodine, which provides a useful option. If you like the taste of seaweed, enjoying it occasionally will provide some iodine. If you don't regularly consume products fortified with iodine, take a non-seaweed supplement of 150µg a day.

Omega-3
If you're not consuming chia seeds, linseed, hemp seeds or walnuts on a daily basis, take an algae oil supplement with around 450mg of EPA and DHA daily.

Selenium
Aim for two Brazil nuts or choose a supplement containing 60–75µg daily.

FAQs
I really hope this has been a helpful overview, and you feel equipped to eat a healthy, balanced plant-based diet. There are three questions that I see a lot, in response to the guidance I give, which I wanted to include for anyone wondering the same things:

How do I navigate a plant-based diet with IBS/bloating?
If you experience gastrointestinal symptoms, or you have been diagnosed with irritable bowel syndrome (known as IBS), increasing plant foods can be easier said than done. With an increase in plant foods, bloating, cramping, and erratic bowel habits can follow for many people. The good news is that our gut can change and adapt based on our dietary patterns. Having said this, it is important to remember that it isn't only food that could be causing your symptoms, so if you have any concerns, speak with your GP before changing your diet. If you are experiencing abdominal symptoms when you eat more plants, try implementing some of the following tips:

- Transition to a plant-based diet more slowly. Gradually increasing the amount of plants in your diet will allow your digestive system to become accustomed to new types, and increased quantities, of high-fibre foods. Over time, the beneficial bacteria in your gut will increase in number and become more efficient at breaking down your food, reducing any difficult symptoms.
- Keep well hydrated to support your tolerance of increased dietary fibre. I generally advise drinking at least 1.5–2 litres of fluid daily.
- Sit upright, eat slowly and chew well. Digestion begins in your mouth.
- If beans and lentils are a problem for you, make sure you soak, rinse and cook them well to improve their digestibility. Canned beans and lentils are already soaked and cooked, so they just need a good rinse before being used in your meal.

Some types of fermentable carbohydrates found in plant foods such as beans and lentils, wheat and some fruits and vegetables can exacerbate gastrointestinal symptoms. These are known as FODMAPs, or fermentable oligosaccharides, disaccharides, monosaccharides and polyols. If you have been diagnosed with IBS and you are struggling with increasing plant foods, consider speaking to a registered dietitian who may recommend the low FODMAP diet plan and will support you to complete it safely and effectively. Despite the short-term symptoms that can occur, long-term high fibre diets are crucial for gut health, which in turn supports many other aspects of health and wellbeing.

Can I be plant-based if I have a very active lifestyle?
If you are an athlete, or have a very active lifestyle, your nutritional needs will increase. Protein requirements may increase from 0.8g to up to 1.2g per kilogram of body weight per

day for endurance athletes, and up to 1.6g for strength athletes. Unless you are training at an elite level, your protein requirements are unlikely to increase significantly from the amount recommended for the healthy population (see page 39).

Many athletes thrive on a plant-based diet due to the abundance of nutrient-dense plant foods that aid energy levels and recovery, but it can take some adjustment. Plant-based diets are naturally lower in energy due to the high fibre and water content of plant foods. For many people on a plant-based diet, and particularly athletes, eating more is required to maintain intake of both macro- and micronutrients.

Aim to eat regularly by including snacks between meals and regular sources of higher-energy plant foods. These could include nuts and nut butters, seeds, bananas, dates, dried fruits, avocado, hummus and starchy carbohydrates. Adding extra foods like tofu, nuts, seeds and soya milk can be helpful for protein. When we are more active, our appetite usually increases too, so you may find that you naturally consume extra energy and protein through simply feeling more hungry.

Is soya safe? I'm confused by the conflicting information.
Soya is absolutely safe, and even beneficial, to consume as part of your balanced plant-based diet. Choose minimally-processed soya foods such as tofu, tempeh, edamame, miso and soya milk and you will be provided with all nine essential amino acids, as well as fibre, calcium and omega-3 fatty acids.

The misunderstanding around soya stems from its phytoestrogen (plant-oestrogen) content, and concerns that it could work in the same way as human oestrogen leading to hormone disruption. No evidence has confirmed these concerns, and alongside the nutritional benefits, soya foods have been found to improve menopausal symptoms, cognitive function and bone health, and reduce risk of diabetes and kidney disease.

Putting it all together

I really hope that Rosie's breakdown of what a balanced diet looks like has been helpful. I always find it comforting to know that the reality is relatively simple – lots of colourful fruit and veg, complex carbs, plant protein, healthy fats and simple supplements. Life does, however, get in the way of the best laid plans and achieving this day in day out can often be harder than it sounds – a concept I really relate to as a busy working mum!

The good news is that while diet plays a fundamental role in our health, it certainly doesn't sit in isolation; it's not the be all and end all. Food is just one part of the puzzle, alongside other lifestyle choices; a fact I think many of us forget far too often. I see it all the time, people are so keen to change what they eat and often look past the other aspects of their lifestyle, all of which play a huge role in our health and the way we feel every day, both mentally and physically. Having experienced this in my own life, I feel passionately about seeing our diet within this context and wanted to delve deeper into that in this chapter. **Rohini Bajekal** felt so well placed to talk us through this, having seen the benefits, both in herself and in her nutrition practice with a range of different clients.

Rohini: why health goes beyond our plate

In my own life, by focusing on my overall lifestyle, I have been able to successfully manage Polycystic Ovary Syndrome (PCOS). This is the most common endocrine disorder worldwide, affecting at least 1 in 10 women with a wide range of reproductive, psychological and metabolic effects. By eating whole plant foods, my energy levels have improved dramatically, along with reducing symptoms such as excess weight gain, acne, anxiety and irregular periods, which are common in PCOS. National and international guidelines agree that health professionals should offer dietary and lifestyle advice along with behavioural strategies as a first step for those diagnosed with PCOS[1,3,4].

In my practice, my clients have also benefited from a holistic approach to improving their health and wellbeing. I have noticed that as you strengthen one lifestyle pillar, the others tend to get stronger too. For example, starting a yoga practice can decrease stress levels, thereby leading you to make more mindful food choices. I encourage clients to implement changes as best they can and to always seek reliable health and nutrition advice. Understanding what matters to the client and how they can practically apply changes in their life helps to create meaningful and sustainable change. It is a huge privilege to play a role in helping my clients achieve their healthful living goals.

Our daily habits have a huge impact on our mental and physical health, far greater than just our genes, profoundly affecting our quality of life, both in the short and long term. These actions can be either health enhancing or disease promoting. We have seen a huge rise in chronic diseases, such as heart disease, type 2 diabetes and certain cancers, to the point that they now make up seven of the world's top 10 causes of death, according to the World Health Organization[5]. Changing our lifestyles can significantly reduce our risk of developing these conditions. The area of lifestyle medicine is one of the most exciting and rapidly growing disciplines within medicine, supported by many peer-reviewed medical studies.

Many national and international guidelines for the prevention and treatment of chronic diseases include these evidence-based lifestyle recommendations. For example, the World Cancer Research Fund recommends regular physical activity, eating a diet rich in whole grains, vegetables, fruit and beans and limiting alcohol consumption for cancer prevention and even after receiving a cancer diagnosis[6]. The benefit of lifestyle medicine is that it addresses the underlying causes of disease while working alongside western medicine. If you require medications or surgery, lifestyle changes can still benefit you. It does not have to be one or the other.

The American College of Lifestyle Medicine (ACLM) succinctly describes this total lifestyle approach using six pillars[7]: nutrition, exercise, stress management, the avoidance of risky substances, sleep and relationships.

1. Nutrition
Nutrition is the cornerstone of optimal wellbeing. When we focus on what we can add to our diet rather than what we're removing, it can be a joyful process. Shireen, Gemma and Alan have all been through why what we eat is so vital to our health, and Rosie has been through what foods to include, so I won't repeat them. Suffice to say that a poor diet is the single leading risk factor for death around the world, with an even greater health burden than smoking. Globally, it's estimated that up to 11 million deaths a year could be prevented with a shift to a plant-based diet – that's a quarter of all deaths[8]. A healthy plant-based diet can lower

inflammation and significantly reduce the risk of chronic diseases such as heart disease[9], type 2 diabetes[10], and several cancers[11]. It can help us maintain healthy blood pressure and cholesterol levels. Our diet is really powerful, but it is not a panacea. There is a huge amount that needs to change at a policy and public health level. We must acknowledge the social determinants of health which include poverty, racism, lack of access to adequate housing and healthy foods, all of which increase a person's risk of health issues.

2. Exercise

Given how much time many of us spend sitting down or being inactive, moving regularly throughout the day is a good way to stay healthy. This means we need to incorporate physical activity (any bodily movement produced by skeletal muscles that requires energy expenditure) and structured exercise (any activity requiring physical effort, carried out to sustain or improve physical fitness). UK guidelines recommend that adults aim for 150 minutes of moderate-intensity exercise per week, or 30 minutes at least five times a week[12]. Even exercising for as little as 15 minutes a day has been shown to reduce the risk of death[13]. Whether it's dancing, strength training, swimming or gardening, regular movement ideally in a form you enjoy is key. Exercise has several proven benefits for the mind and body. It helps maintain a healthy immune system, relieves stress, helps achieve restful sleep and boosts mood. Being physically active also reduces your risk of common chronic diseases such as heart disease and type 2 diabetes, helps maintain a healthy body weight and reduces the rate of bone loss.

If you are new to exercise, it is best to start low and go slow. It can help to set

goals, for example, 'By September 1st, I will walk for 60 minutes at least five days per week.' If you have a desk job, take a break every 20 minutes or so to stretch or do a few simple exercises. Experiment with different types of exercise to find what you prefer and can consistently add into your routine. Listen to your body and build on this every week.

3. Stress management

In the UK, 81% of women admit to regularly feeling overwhelmed[14]. When stress is out of control and chronic, it causes inflammation which contributes to a number of health issues such as anxiety, depression, excess weight gain, insomnia and heart disease. By identifying and acknowledging stress triggers, such as work-related stress or a challenging relationship, you may feel better equipped to address them. Talking openly with a trusted loved one or therapist can make a huge difference. When it comes to stress management, it is important to find what works for you. Try going for a walk with a friend, practising mindfulness, deep breathing exercises or laughing with others to help manage stress levels and build resilience. If you are not sure where to start, setting healthier boundaries in different areas of your life, including time spent on social media, can positively impact your mental health. Practising gratitude and journaling can help you to notice the small, positive moments in your everyday life and challenge negative thought patterns. Remember that rest is a basic human need – one that improves health, immunity and satisfaction. If you continue to feel negatively impacted and unable to cope with stress, it is important to seek help early.

4. Avoidance of risky substances

Certain toxins such as alcohol and tobacco increase stress on the body and impact the function of our immune system. Cigarette smoking and alcohol are both Class 1 carcinogens, which means that they are known to cause cancer. Research consistently shows that drinking any form of alcohol increases a woman's risk of developing breast cancer[15]. Alcohol misuse is also the biggest risk factor for death, ill-health, and disability among 15-49-year-olds in the UK[16]. Counselling is available on the NHS through your doctor and can be helpful when it comes to quitting addictive substances or behaviours along with setting goals. If you plan to cut down, set specific alcohol-free days or commit to a longer challenge. Swap a cigarette for a walk with a friend or warm bath, or an alcoholic drink for a zero-alcohol substitute or sparkling water with lemon.

5. Sleep

Insomnia is thought to affect about a third of people in Western countries at least once a week, with almost twice as many women compared to men affected[17]. It is defined as difficulty in getting to sleep or maintaining sleep, early wakening, or waking up without feeling refreshed despite enough opportunities for sleep. Many of us compromise on prioritising sleep and over time the effects of chronic sleep deprivation can accumulate and negatively impact blood sugar control, weight and blood pressure. Lack of restful sleep can lead to a decreased ability to recover from infection and illness with adverse effects on mental and physical health.

Aim for seven to nine hours of restorative sleep every night. This amount helps with DNA and cell repair, improves mood and reduces stress levels. Too much or too little sleep should be avoided, although there are times when this is unavoidable, for

example with a newborn. Exposure to morning daylight can help improve sleep quality along with regular exercise.

Develop a relaxing bedtime routine by avoiding screens for a couple of hours before you sleep and reducing stimulants, such as alcohol and caffeine. This can help you get a better night's sleep, along with eating a lighter evening meal at least a few hours before going to bed. A warm bath, drinking a caffeine-free herbal tea, listening to calming music, meditating or reading may help you switch off and fall asleep.

6. Relationships

Connecting with others is important for emotional and physical wellbeing. Stay in touch with colleagues, friends and family, and nurture healthy relationships that enrich your life. Community events, volunteering or joining a book club are great ways to make new friends. Find activities you enjoy and meet others, preferably face to face. Learning a new skill or language also helps to keep your brain healthy. People with positive relationships tend to enjoy better health and immunity and even live longer. In contrast, loneliness and isolation are associated with chronic stress and poor health outcomes, especially among individuals already diagnosed with health conditions. Focus on the quality of your relationships rather than the quantity and those who bring out the best in you.

When you start to improve one aspect of your life, you will almost always see benefits in other areas. While lifestyle changes do not guarantee a disease-free life, focusing on what is in your control can be incredibly empowering. Even a few small changes go a long way.

raising plant-based children

raising plant-based children

We're lucky enough to have two gorgeous girls, Skye and May. At the time of publication Skye will have recently turned three and May will be almost two. They're total opposites when it comes to food. One of them eats really well: she runs to the dinner table and gobbles up whatever we make for her. She doesn't really like anything sweet and is the first child I've ever met to refuse all birthday cake, but she'll eat anything savoury and more often than not wants seconds. She loves healthy food – lentils, beans, oats, potatoes, green smoothies, chia pudding and berries. The other is much less of a foodie; she's fussier, mostly unbothered by the idea of meals, no matter what we've made her (bar birthday cake), and much prefers to play than to sit and eat. The lack of interest means mealtimes can, at times, feel pretty stressful. I truly believe they were born this way; they're only 14 months apart in age and were both raised and weaned in exactly the same way, yet their appetites, approach to food and likes/dislikes are so completely different.

I've learnt never to compare them – neither with each other nor with anyone else's children – and to appreciate the fact that they're different and we should embrace that rather than fight it. I have read a lot about fussy eating, and have found that some strategies work and others are much less successful. The biggest take-home though, and the reason I'm starting this section with my experience, is because I truly believe

that there is no one way to feed your children, just as there's no one way to parent them. There's enough pressure on parents already, and comparing how and what your child eats to someone else's child just adds fuel to an already very hot fire! Likewise, this section isn't about persuading you to raise plant-based children, it's about equipping you with the information, in case you need it.

When it comes to what we cook for the girls, the question I'm asked the most is whether we're raising them as vegetarians, totally plant-based or somewhere in between. For now, we've made the decision to be plant-based at home and vegetarian at nursery and with their friends. That balance works really well at the moment. Given that no one around them, most notably their friends at nursery, is entirely plant-based it was really important to me that food didn't become something that ever made them feel separate. Likewise, because one of them is a fussy eater, it felt right to give her more options when she's not with us, to ensure she eats a balanced diet. I know some readers will disagree with this approach and have expected them to be fully plant-based, but transparency is at the heart of what I do and who we are as a brand.

In terms of what they chose to do when they're older – another question I often get asked; that's completely up to them. I'm passionate about educating them on why we've chosen to live and eat the way we do and teaching them to cook, so that they know how to make delicious, nourishing food. Likewise, I have a feeling that by the time they are teenagers, a mostly plant-based diet will be the norm – we've already transitioned to almost 50% of the UK regularly shopping for plant-based options in supermarkets. That being said, how we eat is highly individual and as I hope you've gathered, I don't believe in being dogmatic, so I will respect whatever they choose to do in their lives.

While they're little I just want to give them the most delicious, nourishing food that I can. When they were tiny I had a lot of questions about how to raise plant-based or vegetarian children, wondering how different their diet should be to mine and my husband's, and what were the key things to watch out for. I've had thousands of emails from parents asking about navigating a plant-based or partially plant-based diet for their children, and many more from parents whose teenagers have decided to become vegetarian or fully plant-based and are looking for more resources. So, whatever advice, help or reassurance that you and your family need, I really hope this chapter helps. **Paula Hallam** is the most brilliant paediatric dietician and I've definitely taken a lot from what she's shared.

Paula: plant-based children
According to the Vegan Society, the number of vegans in Great Britain quadrupled between 2014 and 2019. Additionally, a more recent survey by the Vegan Society in May 2021 revealed that 1 in 4 British people had reduced the amount of animal products they were consuming since the start of the COVID-19 pandemic[1]. So, a lot of parents are probably asking themselves the same questions that you are.

These statistics have been mirrored in my own nutrition practice, where I have seen a dramatic increase in the number of families approaching me for nutritional advice for raising their children on a vegan/predominantly plant-based/vegetarian diet.

On a personal note, my own family has turned towards a plant-based diet in the past few years, with our daughters inspiring us to adopt this way of life. I think that a lot of young people are embracing a more 'plant-forward' lifestyle and as these young adults may go on to have families of their own, it follows that they would want to raise their children with the same dietary patterns in mind.

When it comes to feeding our children, optimising their growth and development is the most important factor behind the decisions we make about their nutrition and diet and should be the priority. You may have seen or heard scary headlines in the media, questioning the safety of vegan, vegetarian or plant-based diets for children, so I think the first question to address is that of safety.

Is a vegan, plant-based or vegetarian diet safe for babies and children?
The short answer is, yes! In fact the British Dietetic Association (BDA) says that, 'a balanced vegan diet can be enjoyed by children and adults, including during pregnancy and breastfeeding, if the nutritional intake is well-planned[2].' Plant-based, vegetarian and vegan diets can all be completely safe and adequate for children[3]. As with all diets, the quality and variety of foods offered to children should be carefully considered.

Several professional organisations, including the Academy of Nutrition and

Dietetics[4], the American Academy of Paediatrics[5], the Canadian Paediatric Society[6], Dietitians of Canada[7] and the British Dietetic Association[2] all agree that appropriately planned vegetarian and vegan diets are not only safe but may provide certain health advantages over omnivorous diets.

The Academy of Nutrition and Dietetics's[4] position on the subject is that: 'appropriately planned vegetarian, including vegan, diets are healthful, nutritionally adequate, and may provide health benefits for the prevention and treatment of certain diseases. These diets are appropriate for all stages of the life cycle, including pregnancy, lactation, infancy, childhood, adolescence, older adulthood, and for athletes.'

What does the research say about children's growth?

Research from the Vegetarian and Vegan Children Study published in 2019[8] concluded that vegetarian and vegan diets provided sufficient energy and nutrients to support the growth of young children, as their growth did not differ significantly to children of the same age eating an omnivorous diet. However, it is important to mention that there were a small number of children in the vegetarian and vegan groups of this study whose growth was classified as 'insufficient'. All of these children were either exclusively breastfed for extended periods of time without any solid foods being introduced or had insufficient total energy intakes.

This highlights why it is so important to provide sufficient calories and protein for all children to support their growth and development. Conversely, there was a higher percentage of children in the omnivore diet group that were classified as overweight than in the vegetarian or vegan groups. Another study from the same group – the VeChi Youth

study[9] – involved children aged 6–18 years old and was published in 2021. It concluded that 'a vegetarian, including a vegan, diet can meet the recommended nutrient requirements in childhood and adolescence'. The study also found that the total energy intake did not differ between the groups and that protein intake was more than adequate in all diet groups (vegan, vegetarian and omnivore). The children in the vegan group had the most favourable fat quality intake with the highest intakes of polyunsaturated and monounsaturated fats and the lowest intake of saturated fat[9]. The vegan group also had the *highest* intakes of fibre, vitamins E, C and B1, magnesium and iron, and the *lowest* intakes of: saturated fat (this is a good thing!), vitamins B2 and B12 (without supplements), calcium and iodine. But the vegan children had the *highest* intakes of vitamin B12 when supplements were taken into account[9]. This illustrates the importance of vitamin B12 supplementation in vegan children (it is essential for both adults and children on a plant-based or predominantly plant-based diet). The vegetarian children also had low vitamin B12 intakes in this study and the authors recommended that vegetarian children should also receive a vitamin B12 supplement.

The vegan children had the lowest intakes of calcium but none of the diet groups achieved the recommended calcium intake (vegan children had calcium intakes of less than half the recommended amount; vegetarian children had calcium intakes of just over half the recommended amount and omnivore children had calcium intakes that were two thirds of the recommended amount)[9]. Care should be taken to ensure adequate calcium intake in *all* children and adolescents to avoid any detrimental effects on bone health (as well as vitamin D supplementation to improve calcium absorption).

Similarly with iodine, the vegan children had the lowest intakes but none of the diet groups had adequate intakes, even in the omnivore group[9]. The richest sources of iodine in the UK diet are dairy products, white fish and eggs[10]. Some dairy alternative drinks and yoghurts are fortified with iodine, but always check the nutrition label to be sure. If you or your child is vegan, the most reliable way of ensuring an adequate intake of iodine is by taking a supplement (see page 58).

In conclusion, vegetarian and vegan diets can provide sufficient energy and nutrients to support the growth of children and adolescents. Care should be taken to provide sufficient energy and nutrient-dense foods, especially to babies and young children, and supplementation is essential for vegan children (see pages 54–59 for information on recommended supplements).

Nutritional considerations

The needs of children do vary a little, from infants to teenagers. Below you'll find a breakdown of each age range and their specific requirements.

0–6 months

For the first six months of your baby's life, breast milk is the ideal food for all babies including babies of vegan/plant-based/vegetarian mums[11]. Any amount of breast milk is beneficial for your baby, even if you cannot breastfeed exclusively. Breast milk provides all the nutrients your baby needs for the first six months of life, except vitamin D (see page 54).

Breastfeeding mums do not need to eat a specific/special diet, but it is important they ensure that they are eating a balanced diet with sufficient calories/energy to support the formation of breast milk. It is estimated that around 25% of a breastfeeding mum's energy intake – around 450–500 calories per day – is used to form breastmilk[12], so they may need an additional 1 or 2 snacks per day.

The UK recommended intake for calcium for breastfeeding mums is very high at 1250mg per day, which is 550mg higher than the 700mg calcium per day recommended for female adults[11]. Breastfeeding women need to aim to include plenty of calcium-rich foods in their diet, such as:

- Milk, yoghurt and cheese (if eating dairy products).
- Calcium-fortified plant-based drinks and yoghurts.
- Calcium-set tofu*, e.g. Cauldron.
- Calcium-fortified breads and cereals.
- Green leafy vegetables that are low in oxalates** (broccoli, pak choi, watercress, kale, Brussel sprouts).
- Oranges and dried figs.
- Nuts, such as almonds, Brazil nuts, hazelnuts and pistachio nuts.
- Sesame seeds and tahini.

* You can look out for the words 'calcium chloride' (E509) or 'calcium sulphate' (E516) on the label to check if the tofu you buy is calcium-set. If the label says 'nigari' it is not a good source of calcium.

** Not all green vegetables are good sources of calcium as oxalates can inhibit the absorption of calcium. Spinach is not a good source of calcium, as it is high in oxalates and therefore the calcium within spinach is very poorly absorbed (only around 5% is absorbed).

Important note: some breastfeeding women may need a calcium supplement if they are unable to include a variety of the above foods. Please speak to a Registered Dietician.

Vitamin A requirements also increase during breastfeeding[13]. Breastfeeding women need to include plenty of carotenoid-rich foods, such as pumpkin, sweet potato, carrots, peppers and green leafy vegetables. Carotenoids are the plant-based precursors to vitamin A, which means that they will be converted to vitamin A in the body. If you include dairy and eggs in your diet, you can also obtain vitamin A from cheese, full-fat cow's milk and eggs.

What other options are there for feeding my baby? Other options for feeding your baby in the first six months of life, if breastfeeding is not possible, include donor breast milk and infant formula milk. There is currently no fully vegan infant formula available in the UK. There are certain vegan brands of infant formula available from mainland Europe, such as Premiriz, which is based on hydrolysed rice protein[14]. Soya infant formula (SMA Soya Infant Formula is the only brand of soya formula currently available in the UK) is an option for plant-based families and can be used safely from birth to support your baby's growth and development[15, 16]. However, SMA Soya Infant Formula is not considered fully vegan as the source of vitamin D is from lanolin in sheep's wool, but it is considered vegetarian[17]. (See page 61 for more about soya.)

Please speak with your health professional if you are planning to feed your baby soya infant formula under the age of six months, as the NHS currently has a precautionary approach and does not recommend soya infant formula for babies under this age (unless advised by a health professional). There are certain circumstances when soya infant formula is *not* appropriate for babies[18]. These include: babies born prematurely (at 36 weeks' gestation or earlier), babies with kidney problems, and babies with

congenital hypothyroidism (as soya can interfere with the absorption of the medication). In addition, some children with cow's milk protein allergy may not be able to tolerate soya protein[19] – please discuss this with your health professional.

It is absolutely essential that babies are *never* fed any homemade formulas, such as those made from boiled rice water, under any circumstances. This is because they are nutritionally inadequate and are not safe for babies and young children as they do not provide sufficient energy, protein, fats, vitamins or minerals to support their growth and development. There has sadly been severe cases of malnutrition and even death in some babies who have been fed homemade formulas.

Supplements for babies aged 0–6 months In the UK, the NHS recommends that all breastfed babies are supplemented with 8.5–10µg vitamin D per day from birth (in addition to breastfeeding mums taking a vitamin D supplement, as below)[20]. Formula-fed babies do not need a supplement until they are drinking less than 500ml of infant formula per 24 hours. This is because infant formula is supplemented with these vitamins already.

Supplements during breastfeeding In the UK, the NHS recommends that all breastfeeding mums (regardless of diet choice) consider a vitamin D supplement of 10µg per day[21].

Additional supplements recommended for plant-based breastfeeding mums[22]
- **Vitamin B12** 10–25µg per day or 1000µg twice per week.
- **Iodine** 150–200µg per day.
- **DHA/EPA** combined (plant-based micro algae): 400-500mg per day, containing at least 250mg DHA.

6–12 months

A baby's first year of life is a period of rapid growth – babies typically triple their birth weight and grow an average of 25cm in their first year[23]. In order to support their growth and development, babies need nutrient- and energy-dense foods. Once babies are around six months old and are showing the correct signs of developmental readiness (including being able to sit up with minimal support and hold their heads in a stable position), solid foods can be introduced.

When introducing solids to your baby, iron-rich foods should be a priority. This is because iron requirements increase from seven months of age[24] due to the fact that the iron stores that babies are born with start to decrease from six months of age. Additionally, breast milk does not contain much iron[25], so it is vitally important to source iron from food. Examples of iron-rich foods include:

- all types of beans
- all types of lentils
- chickpeas, hummus and tahini
- nuts and seeds (including nut/seed butters or ground nuts)
- iron-fortified cereals and breads
- tofu and edamame beans
- dark green leafy vegetables
- seeds, such as chia, flax and hemp
- quinoa and oats

As the absorption of iron from plant-based sources is not as good as the absorption from meat-based sources (known as bioavailability), it is important to pair these iron-rich foods with vitamin-C-rich foods as vitamin C increases the absorption of iron by two to four times[26]. Onion and garlic have also been shown to increase the absorption of iron significantly[27]. Examples of vitamin-C-rich foods include peppers, potatoes, tomatoes, kiwi fruit, strawberries, raspberries, blackcurrants, broccoli, Brussels sprouts and citrus fruits.

Another important consideration when introducing solids to your baby is to make sure you are offering energy-dense foods. Do not be afraid of fats! As babies are growing rapidly we need to ensure that every bite of food is packed with important nutrients, such as iron, but also high-calorie foods rich in fats, such as avocado, nut butters, tahini, olive paste (check for added salt), vegetables cooked in olive or avocado oil and seeds, such as chia, flax or hemp.

Adapting recipes for weaning You can easily adapt the food that you are eating so that it is appropriate for your baby – this saves you both time and money. The important points to remember are that your baby's food should have no added salt or sugar, should not include any low-fat foods or excessive amounts of fibre (introduce gradually to babies).

Some practical examples include
1. If making a soup or stew, take a portion out for your baby before adding any stock/salt.

2. If you are vegetarian and consume dairy products, always use full-fat milk/yoghurt/cheese.

3. If roasting vegetables, use olive oil or avocado oil and set some aside for your baby before adding any salt. You can still use herbs, garlic and spices (though of course, not hot chilies!) for your baby, you only need to avoid added salt.

Throughout the book recipes that can be adapted for children have been highlighted with a 'Tip for Tinies' note.

Supplements for babies aged 6-12 months From six months of age, the Department of Health in the UK recommends a supplement of vitamins A, C and D for all breastfed babies (not only vegan/vegetarian babies) and once formula-fed babies are drinking less than 500ml formula per day[20].

For vegan and predominantly plant-based babies, it would also be prudent to start a vitamin B12 supplement at this stage. Breastfed babies will obtain their vitamin B12 from breast milk (as long as mum is supplementing; see page 54) but when babies are eating three meals per day and drinking less breast milk/formula, a vitamin B12 supplement of 2.5–5µg per day is recommended[22].

Toddlers (1–4 years)
The toddler years can be a fun time, watching your child grow and discover new things around them can be very rewarding for parents. Toddlers start gaining independence and autonomy and it can be so refreshing to see your child capable of doing more for themselves, but equally it can also be frustrating if they start refusing foods that they had previously enjoyed!

One of the things you may notice about your toddler is that their growth slows down, when compared to the first 12 months of life[29]. This has a knock-on effect on their appetite and your 9-month-old who previously gobbled up everything you offered may have turned into an 18-month-old who only eats a few bites of a meal! Let me reassure you that this is completely normal. At this age, it is important to have a structured meal and snack routine in place, so that your toddler is offered food approximately every 2–3 hours across the day. Three meals and two snacks per day works well for most children and can help ensure that your toddler is not becoming over-hungry. For further tips on managing fussy eating, see page 59).

Iron requirements continue to be high (relative to body weight) throughout the toddler years and so it is important to continue offering iron-rich foods at most meals (paired with vitamin C-rich foods to aid absorption). Examples include:
- Hummus with peppers
- Black beans and tomatoes
- Porridge with strawberries or kiwi
- Tofu and potatoes

Calcium requirements[24] are lower than that in the first year of life at 350mg calcium from 1–3 years of age (in the UK). This can easily be provided by 300ml (around two small cups) full fat cow's milk if your family includes dairy products or 300ml fortified soya/pea/oat-based dairy drink alternative. During childhood, calcium requirements increase steadily to 450mg per day for 4–6 year olds and 550mg per day for 7–10 year olds[24]. Continuing to include a fortified plant-based dairy alternative (or cow's milk if vegetarian) can be a useful source of calcium for children, as well as offering a wide variety of plant foods that are naturally rich in calcium, such as calcium-set tofu, broccoli, oranges, figs, almond butter and tahini.

Supplements for toddlers From around one year of age, your toddler may need certain supplements, depending on whether your family is vegetarian, vegan or predominantly plant-based. During the first year of life, breast milk or formula milk provides an important source of many nutrients, but you should supplement vitamins A, C and D (for all breastfed babies from 6 months of age and babies drinking less than 500ml formula) as well as starting vitamin B12 from around 6–8 months of age (as specified above).

From one year of age, additional supplements for vegan children include iodine and DHA[28]. See the table at the end of the section on page 60 for supplement recommendations and dosages for different age groups.

Adolescents (11–18 years)

Adolescence is a time of rapid growth and remarkable change. Alongside the unique emotional and physical changes of adolescence, teens also have unique nutritional requirements. During adolescence the growth rate is the second fastest over a lifetime, the only other time it is greater, is during the first year of life[23,30]. As a result of this rapid growth, energy requirements increase. Other nutrient requirements that increase during adolescence include:

Calcium requirements increase during adolescence in order to support bone growth. There is a jump from 550mg calcium per day for 7–10 year olds, to 800mg/1000mg (girls/boys respectively) per day from 11–18 years[24]. It is a good idea to encourage your teen to include a fortified plant-based dairy alternative (PBDA) drink in their diet to improve calcium intake. Aim for three cups of fortified PBDA drink per day – these can be included over cereal/porridge as well as in smoothies and drinks. If your family is vegetarian, aim to offer three cups of cow's milk or yoghurt per day.

There are also many fortified PBDA yoghurts available, as well as the non-dairy calcium-rich foods mentioned in the section for breastfeeding mums, such as calcium-set tofu, certain green vegetables, oranges, dried figs, fortified cereals and breads, which can all contribute to calcium intake.

Vitamin D is also important for calcium absorption. In the UK we don't obtain enough sunlight at the optimum wavelength during the autumn and winter months, so it is important to consider a vitamin D supplement of 10µg per day for all adolescents and adults during these months[31].

Iron Another micronutrient of importance during this period is iron, especially in adolescent girls as iron requirements increase significantly as a result of menstruation. There is an increase in iron requirements from just under 9mg per day in 7–10 year olds (girls and boys), to almost 15mg per day for menstruating girls and just over 11mg for boys[24]. Offering iron-rich foods at most meals will help to ensure that these requirements are met, alongside pairing iron-rich foods with vitamin C rich foods to improve their absorption (see page 55 for examples). As teens are eating larger portions of foods than younger children, driven by their hunger, they will be receiving more iron from foods.

Protein Adolescents need around 40–55g protein per day[24] depending on their age and gender (a teen athlete may need slightly more). Offering a variety of protein-rich plant-based foods across the day, will easily cover your teen's protein requirements. Excellent plant-based sources of protein include all beans, lentils, chickpeas and hummus, soya beans/edamame, tofu, tempeh, soya/pea based dairy alternatives, nuts, seeds, quinoa, oats and Quorn. If your teen is vegetarian, eggs and dairy products can also contribute to their protein intake. Your teen's protein needs can easily be met on a plant-based diet. Some examples include:

- Toast (2 slices) with 2 tablespoons of peanut butter = 16g protein
- 600ml soya/pea-based dairy alternative = 18g protein
- Tofu and noodle stir-fry = 13g protein
- Lentil and black bean burrito = 13g protein

TOTAL = 60g protein

Supplements for plant-based children

For vegan and predominantly plant-based children, the following supplements are recommended (in addition to vitamins A, C and D).

Vitamin B12

All vegan and predominantly plant-based children (from six months of age) and adults should take a vitamin B12 supplement because vitamin B12 is only found in animal-based and fortified foods. Vegans who do not consume fortified foods or a vitamin B12 supplement on a daily basis are at a high risk of vitamin B12 deficiency[9]. The amounts recommended vary depending on age (see table on page 60). Vegetarians may also wish to consider supplementing with vitamin B12 as some studies have shown low vitamin B12 status among vegetarians. [9]

Iodine

Studies have consistently shown that many children have low intakes of iodine, regardless of diet choice. Vegan, followed by vegetarian children tend to have the lowest intakes of iodine in studies[9].

The main sources of iodine in the UK diet are dairy products, eggs, white fish and seafood. Iodised salt is another potential source of iodine but salt does not routinely have iodine added to it in the UK[32]; in addition, the UK government recommendations are to reduce salt intake for public health reasons, therefore iodised salt is not recommended as a reliable source of iodine for adults or children.

Seaweed is a concentrated source of iodine, but as the iodine content of some seaweeds can be excessive (particularly in brown seaweed, such as kelp), seaweed should not be offered to children and pregnant/breast-feeding women more than once per week[33] and not offered at all to babies under the age of 12 months[18].

Many plant-based dairy alternative drinks are fortified with iodine (as well as calcium and vitamins, check the label). Your child may need an iodine supplement, depending on how much fortified dairy alternative they drink and the level of iodine fortification within the drink. Please speak with your health professional if you'd like further guidance or if you are unsure if your child needs a supplement. See the table on page 60 for the amounts of iodine recommended at different ages.

Omega-3 fats (ALA, DHA and EPA)

Omega-3 fats are a type of polyunsaturated fat and ALA (alpha-linolenic acid) is called an 'essential fat' as our bodies cannot make it 'from scratch', so we need to obtain ALA from the food we eat. ALA is present in many plant foods such as walnuts, chia seeds, flax seeds, hemp seeds and their oils, as well as small amounts in tofu and edamame. ALA is what we call the 'parent' or 'precursor' fatty acid and it is converted through a series of steps to DHA (docosahexanoic acid) and EPA (eicosapentanoic acid), which are considered the 'active' forms.

Research has shown that DHA is a critical nutrient for babies and young children up to the age of two years, as it is essential for brain and eye development. Omega-3 fats, including DHA, have an anti-inflammatory role in the body and studies have shown that DHA is important for baby's ability to learn, remember and these essential fats also support normal IQ[34].

Babies receive these omega-3 fats from their mother before birth (across the placenta) and after birth from breast milk, if mum eats enough omega-3 fats in her diet[35]. For fully plant-based children not eating any fish, they are unlikely to get enough DHA from the food they eat and an algae oil supplement is recommended.

The reason oily fish are high in DHA and EPA is because they eat algae that contains DHA and EPA. So giving your child an algal oil supplement is like cutting out the middle man!

There is some debate as to whether children over the age of two and adults need to supplement DHA and EPA directly, but many people choose to take them regularly because of their potential benefits for the brain and the heart[36]. It is still important to include good sources of ALA in the diet, such as walnut, chia, flax and hemp seeds. For children and babies under the age of two years, as well as pregnant and breastfeeding mums who do not eat oily fish, a supplement of DHA and EPA is highly recommended.

FAQs

What if my child is a fussy eater?

Fussy eating is very common in toddlers with up to 50% of toddlers experiencing some form of fussy eating[37]. Rest assured, you are not alone! Fussy eating is a developmental phase that most children go through. It usually starts at around 18 months of age with a peak at about 3 years. By 5–6 years of age most children 'come out the other side'[38]. Don't worry, there are many strategies and tips available to help you manage your fussy eater . . .

1. Develop a routine for mealtimes and snacks The key to a successful routine for meals and snacks is TIMING. Aim to offer your toddler an 'eating opportunity' every 2–3 hours. Try not to let your child graze all day as they will not learn about hunger/fullness cues.

2. Try to recognise signals for when your toddler has had enough to eat – they are telling you they have had enough when they:
- Say no!
- Keep their mouth shut
- Turn their head away
- Push away a spoon or fork
- Hold food in their mouth
- Spit food out

3. Check your toddler's milk intake
Between 1 and 3 years of age, toddlers need a maximum of 350ml of milk (cow's milk or fortified dairy alternative) per day, less if taking other dairy products like yoghurt and cheese, to meet their calcium requirements. Milk is more like a food than a drink as it is very filling, so try not to offer your toddler too much milk.

4. Offer small portions so that your child is not overwhelmed by the amount of food in front of them.

5. Eat together as often as possible
Focus on making mealtimes a positive and relaxed experience for your children.

6. Get creative Start cooking with your children and involve them in food preparation as much as possible. Exposure to foods helps with acceptance of these foods. Growing herbs is a great way to get children curious about flavours.

7. Take the pressure off! Research has shown that bribing, coercing or forcing children to eat does not work to support their acceptance of foods in the long term[38]. Instead, use the 'division of responsibility' where you decide what you offer to your child and they decide how much they eat.

summary of recommended supplements for plant-based children

(*in addition to vitamins A, C and D for all under 5s)

Nutrient	Recommended Daily Quantity
Vitamin B12	
Breastfeeding mums	10–25μg (but some references say up to 100–250μg per day)**
7–12 months of age	2.5μg*
1–3 years of age	2.5–5μg*
4–8 years of age	5μg*
9–13 years of age	10–25μg*
14+ years of age	25–50μg*

*Plant Based Health professionals UK
**Nourish by Shah and Davis

Iodine (combination of WHO and the Vegan Society (UK) recommendations)	
Breastfeeding mums	150–200μg
1–3 years of age	50–70μg
4–6 years of age	100μg
7–12 years of age	120μg
13+ years (and adults)	150μg

DHA/EPA (WHO/FAO 2008)	
Breastfeeding mums	400–500mg DHA + EPA
1–2 years	100mg DHA
2–4 years	100–150mg DHA + EPA
4–6 years	150–200mg DHA + EPA
6–10 years	200–250mg DHA + EPA
11+ years	250mg DHA + EPA

How can my child get enough calcium without dairy?

It is a common myth that children must drink cow's milk in order to obtain enough calcium. Calcium is essential for bone health, but there are also other nutrients such as protein, vitamin D, vitamin K and magnesium that are equally important for bone health[39]. Weight-bearing exercise is another important aspect of bone health.

Calcium does not need to come from dairy products. There are plenty of excellent plant-based sources, such as:

- Calcium-fortified plant based drinks and yoghurts.
- Calcium-set tofu (see page 53).
- Calcium-fortified breads and cereals.
- Some green leafy vegetables (kale broccoli, bok choi, watercress, Brussels sprouts).
- Oranges and dried figs.

- Certain nuts, particularly almonds.
- Sesame seeds and tahini.

Is soya safe for my child?

Yes! A systematic review and meta-analysis (very high-quality research evidence) from 2014 looked at the combined data from 35 studies on the safety of soya-milk formulas. They found that 'patterns of growth, bone health, metabolic, reproductive endocrine, immune and neurological functions are similar to those fed human milk or cow's milk formula'[16]. The British Dietetic Association Paediatric Specialist Group Position's statement on the use of infant formulas based on soya protein states: 'vegan mothers [...] should be strongly encouraged to breastfeed, but if they are unable to breastfeed or choose not to do so, soy formula would be the appropriate choice.'

I think this is very reassuring and you can safely offer soya foods including fortified soya milk to your children. In fact, some research has shown that not only is soya not harmful, it is in fact beneficial for the prevention of some chronic diseases such as certain types of cancer[40].

What is the best plant-based dairy alternative drink for my toddler?

There is no 'perfect' plant-based dairy alternative (PBDA) drink out there for toddlers, but typically soya or pea-based options are the most nutritious for toddlers. Oat-based alternatives are another option, but they are lower in protein than soya/pea-based options.

When trying to choose a dairy alternative, consider the following:

- Check the energy and protein content of the PBDA drink as many are very low in calories and protein. Ideally look for a PBDA that is around 50 calories (or more) per 100ml and contains 2-3g protein.
- Look for PBDA drinks that are fortified (organic versions are not) with calcium, vitamin D, vitamin B12 and iodine. Vitamin B2 would also be useful. These micronutrients (except for vitamin D) are all typically present in cow's milk.
- For older children, you can use PBDA drinks that are slightly lower in calories (from 30–40 calories per 100ml, equivalent to skimmed/semi-skimmed milk) and I would recommend continuing the use of a fortified PBDA drink throughout childhood to provide useful sources of calcium, iodine and vitamins.

Please note that breast milk is the ideal milk for toddlers – breastfeeding is recommended until two years and beyond by the World Health Organization. So if you are able and happy to continue breastfeeding beyond a year of age, that is a great option and you don't necessarily need to introduce an additional calcium-rich drink, as long as they are feeding around three to four times per day and eating one or two calcium-rich foods.

How can I make sure my toddler is getting enough protein?

Aim to offer your child a variety of plant foods, including those rich in protein, such as all beans, lentils, chickpeas, nuts, seeds, tofu and soya products, alongside wholegrain foods. Babies and young children actually don't need very much protein to grow and thrive. A toddler needs around 15g protein per day, which could be provided by:

- 200ml soya milk = 5-6g protein +
- 1 slice wholemeal toast with 1 tablespoon of peanut butter = 8g protein +
- Pasta with pesto = 3-4g protein

TOTAL = 16–18g protein

how to change your diet

how to change your diet

I've always felt that it's one thing to be told you need to eat more healthily, it's another to understand why that's so important, which I hope you now do, but it's a whole different ball game to apply those learnings. As a society we're quick to blame ourselves for not being able to implement healthy habits instantly, for not seeing a change through, nor instantaneously becoming the person we may aspire to be. As far as I can see, this mindset is incredibly unhelpful. Let's be honest, making a genuine change in our lives is really hard, and I think we should be more realistic about that.

I certainly found altering my diet very difficult to begin with. I wanted to make the change, I knew I had to do something, but it felt so unfamiliar, I had to shift all my automatic responses. The change didn't feel seamless until my new meals, shopping lists, snacks, and ways of being were the default, at which point living a healthy life became incredibly easy and enjoyable, to the point that I can't remember doing it any differently. That took months though, not days. So, if that's where you are, then please don't feel alone. To help you, I wanted to include some support from a psychologist, someone with first-hand experience of people struggling to make a change in their own lives. I first spoke to **Shahroo Izadi** four years ago and was blown away by her gentle, compassionate approach and her resolute emphasis on the fact that it's impossible to make a change without

shifting your mindset first, and that shift has to be positive.

Before we delve into Shahroo's insights and a few practical exercises, I wanted to share a tip from each of the healthcare professionals that we've spoken to, to better understand what shift helped them embrace a change more easily.

For me, it was realising that whatever changes I made in my life, I had to love them and actively want to do them. It was no good saying 'I should do this'. If I didn't love it, then I wasn't going to keep doing it and I needed to embrace that. I love food, so everything I ate had to be delicious, it couldn't feel like a compromise. I accepted I really didn't like some 'healthy' foods and that was more than okay.

Shireen
Remembering my why. For me it was about living more kindly and compassionately. Social support has also been really important and I transitioned to a vegan diet with my two sisters, which made it much more enjoyable and therefore sustainable. We explored new recipes and food options together and shared that new knowledge.

Gemma
Focussing on *why* I wanted to make changes was crucial. After I went fully plant-based, I was pleased to bring my cholesterol down, and pleased that the

pain in my knees when I was running had melted away. But if I am honest, the thing that really made me stick to it was deeper than that – I was widening my circle of compassion. I made helping my patients improve their health my career. Seeing my patients' incredible health transformations has been so fulfilling. Knowing I was also making a compassionate choice for animals through what I chose to put on my plate also really helped to keep me going, coupled with the importance of my choice for the environment.

Alan

My top tip is to share your food. When you've made the switch to a healthier plant-based approach, sharing your food with friends and loved ones becomes such a positive experience. Once they've enjoyed a delicious plant-based meal they will understand why you are so enthusiastic about this way of eating. When my family and I made the switch we always made sure to cook extra and to invite some people over.

Rosie

Embrace abundance. It is all too easy to focus on the foods you are trying to reduce or remove when changing your diet. The wonderful thing about a plant-based diet is that you can instead focus on the abundance of colourful plant foods that you can have. I love getting creative with new recipes, new foods, and new ways of cooking. By approaching the transition with curiosity, our journeys will become exciting and joyful, and I've found that any foods I thought I couldn't live without have simply been crowded out by new and delicious taste sensations.

Rohini

For me, it's been about improving my cooking skills. This helped me build confidence and allowed me to try

different cuisines from around the world that have always celebrated plants. I love cooking for my family and friends and surprising them with delicious plant-based meals.

Paula

For us as a family, starting gradually really helped. This stopped me from feeling too overwhelmed versus going 'all in' from the start. We are still not fully plant-based and I am 100 per cent okay with that! I think it is very important to be flexible, especially with children.

Shahroo: why kindness is the secret to change

Underestimating the difficulties that can come with truly embedding a new routine is one of the biggest mistakes we can make when hoping to make sustained, meaningful changes.

It's the decisions we make in moments of challenge that determine whether or not we stay on track with new behaviours for long enough to create a new default 'way'. The problem is, so often when we've decided to change our habits, we unhelpfully approach the process from a place of punishment, extremes and disappointment in ourselves for finding it difficult (or for not having changed already).

Many of us have come to assume that a combination of beating ourselves up, bootcamp-style plans, and a genuine desire to change will be enough to make us practise a new routine until it becomes a no-brainer. Armed with all the information and guidance in this book, it's natural to want to dedicate the entirety of our energy to things like selecting the most appealing recipes to try, designing colour-coded rotas, overhauling cupboards and creating new shopping lists.

Unfortunately, this purely practical approach to making changes (one that neglects to consider things like a mindset and self-care) can sometimes set us up for failure by resulting in a series of false starts that eventually leave us feeling disillusioned with our unrealistic plans, as well as disappointed with ourselves for not being able to keep them up despite being in possession of all the information and guidance we needed.

The good news is, we can absolutely avoid this. All we need to make our habits stick is a 'kindness toolkit' of very simple personal development exercises and aides that help us see to see our plans through. Ones that increase the likelihood of our new habits feeling realistic, enjoyable and permanent. Ones that teach us how to treat ourselves with the same compassion and consideration that we usually reserve for the people we love.

The *great* news is, the same tools and insights that can help us to embed a new eating or wellbeing routine can also be re-used to help us to navigate any life transition. That's because they're designed to support us in getting to know ourselves better and believing in ourselves more every day – in any and all areas of our lives. All we need to do for them to be effective is re-think our definition of kindness when it comes to doing difficult things.

Overcoming self-doubt

That rethinking of the word kindness means seeing it as backing yourself. When we're trying to do something challenging (like create new lifestyle habits), it's common for self-doubt to creep in at times. It's easy when we're feeling overwhelmed with lots of new choices on a testing day to forget that we've navigated far more difficult things than the decision we're facing in that moment.

So often, when we are proud of ourselves for achieving something, we quickly normalise that feeling; moving on to the next challenge and starting to see the negatives in the destination we once doubted we could even reach. Neglecting to process what we've managed to do in the past deprives us of an opportunity to feel more ambitious with the goals we set for our futures.

Against the landscape of a busy day, it can feel impossible to bring to the forefront of our minds all the reasons we are more than capable of making the difficult choices we'll be glad we made tomorrow.

That's where visual motivational aids can step in and help. Imagine if, as soon as you started to believe that a new challenge was too difficult for you handle in any life area, you could immediately glance at hard evidence to show you why you're mistaken (and should therefore rethink your next choice).

This first exercise will help you to create just that. Not only does it feel great to complete, but when you're finished, it's going to become a visual reminder in the palm of your hands that helps you to stay on track with your plans.

10-minute written exercise: 'I've got this'

You can use either a notepad and pen, phone or laptop. At the top of your page, note down the title, 'I've got this'.

Reflect on – and write down – all the difficult things you've managed to do and get through in every area of your life up until now. Consider the things that you've achieved and difficult periods you've navigated. Note down everything you've done in the past to demonstrate how capable, strong and resilient you are. The things you're proud of yourself for. The aspects of your life that 15-year old you would love to know you managed to create.

Once you've finished, read through your list slowly and take in how it feels to look at it all written down in one place. Ask yourself whether it looks like the description of someone who is incapable of doing difficult things.

Make sure the list is kept somewhere you can access it throughout the day. Whenever you start doubting your abilities in any area of your life, simply commit to reading your 'I've got this' reminder.

Once you've completed this exercise, it can help to set a weekly reminder or alarm on your phone (perhaps on a Sunday evening), reminding you to spend just five minutes reflecting on that week and adding anything you're proud of yourself for having done or got through. Perhaps include new healthy choices you've managed to make despite a stressful day; the fact that you managed to use social media less; or that you carved out time for a walk every day despite it raining.

When you get into the habit of populating this list, you'll naturally start to notice opportunities when you can set yourself a little challenge, just because you're excited to write it down. Over time, the process of collecting new evidence (and using old evidence to get there) will reinforce itself and you'll remember how great it feels to pleasantly surprise yourself.

Making self-care unconditional

It's common to think that we'll reward ourselves with new hobbies, acts of self-care or joyous activities once we've achieved a desired goal or managed to make a big change in our lives, but not only do we deserve to show ourselves

kindness immediately (regardless of what goals we may be trying to achieve), being as nice as possible to ourselves is a useful way to help us change our habits.

Put plainly, change can be difficult, and doing hard things becomes easier when we pepper our day with things that make us feel more calm, positive and resilient. It's important to give ourselves regular signals and reminders that our bodies, minds and quality of life matter – right now, regardless of our plans and missions.

10-minute written exercise: self-care

Imagine you've already made all the changes you want to make to your lifestyle. Using either a notepad and pen, phone or laptop, write down all the things you intend to do for yourself as a reward, or because you associate those things with being 'a new improved' person? It can be anything from lighting that fancy candle you've been keeping for a special occasion, drinking enough water, finally booking that holiday or becoming more boundaried with colleagues and loved ones.

Go through that list and for each point, ask yourself how many of those things you're perfectly capable (and deserving) of doing now. Commit to trying them one at a time and notice how much more resilient and worthy you feel!

If, while you're completing this exercise, you start feeling 'selfish', please remember that taking care of yourself and doing things that make you feel positive and calm are in the interest of everyone around you. Pouring from an empty cup to support and interact with others is difficult enough when you're not also trying to create new habits. Do whatever you can to cushion your new eating plan between acts of self-care for

All we need is a 'kindness toolkit' – simple exercises and aids that help us see our plans through and increase the likelihood that our habits feel realistic.

your mind and body throughout the day, however small they may be. They're a reminder that your enjoyment and goals matter as much as anyone else's.

Speak to yourself like someone you love

When we're supporting the people we love in doingsomething challenging (like changing their habits and routines), we don't tell them to give up when they're faced with a test. We don't tell them they've blown it when they're fallen off-track; nor do we indulge their predictable justifications to 'start on Monday' in order to swerve the inevitable moments of discomfort involved in any transition. We remind them of their reasons to change. We tell them that we believe in them and help them to see how worthy they are of doing difficult things. We give them positive, common-sense advice and ask how we can best support them. When they do something they're not happy with, we encourage them to learn from it, forgive themselves and move on. We're kind but firm; simultaneously advising against the easy option and compassionately reminding them they can do hard things.

Despite knowing what messages motivate people to make the wisest choices, it's amazing how many of us struggle to take our own advice.

Learning to speak to ourselves differently can play a powerful role in helping us to create new habits and

push through in those moments when we want to throw in the towel and revert back to the (ultimately unwanted, but comfortable) status quo. If we can work towards developing a 'soundtrack' that is more fair, kind and helpful, the resulting shifts in our behaviour can be transformational. Over time, we can learn to coach ourselves to stay on track when we need motivation the most.

The good news is, we already know the messages that motivate, because we know how to support the people we love to achieve *their* goals. We simply need to turn that script on ourselves and believe, over time, that we deserve to hear the same things.

Trying out simple exercises like the ones opposite can help us gently, compassionately and curiously tune in to our current soundtrack, and begin to notice the things we say to ourselves when we most need a pep-talk.

If, once we start listening in, we notice that the things we're hearing seem harsher and more unwise than anything we'd say to someone else, we can gently start to debate, fact-check and update them. The good news is, one fantastic way to quickly turn up the volume on our internal dialogue is to try and do something challenging (like implement a new wellbeing plan).

A lot of us are surprised to learn when we do listen in, that the messages we give ourselves are not only extreme, outdated, unkind and unhelpful (things like 'I've blown it', 'I'm stupid just like my teacher said', etc), they're also very often just untrue. Many of has have internalised 'truths' about ourselves from childhood that now inform the assumptions we make about who we are and what we're capable of as adults. We've never given ourselves the opportunity to fact-check them at different stages, despite the landscape of our lives shifting considerably.

Awareness practice

The next time you feel tempted to neglect your plan of change (or you've already fallen off it and are struggling to get back on track), pause for a moment to listen to what you're telling yourself. Are you making justifications that perhaps you wouldn't let a loved one get away with? Are you underestimating yourself and forgetting all the things you've managed to do that are harder than making the unfamiliar, difficult choice right now (the one you'll be happy you made tomorrow)?

Choosing to listen in with non-judgmental curiosity can be a real game-changer. Once you start to notice the unhelpful messages, you can practise gently debating them before letting them inform and dictate your next move. The 'I've Got This' list on pages 66–67 can help to support this practice. Whenever you hear a self-limiting belief, choose to glance at your list for suggestions of ways you can begin to disprove the outdated message.

10-minute written exercise: championing ourselves

Another exercise that can us that can help us to develop a fairer, kinder, more helpful internal soundtrack involves noticing the difference between how we support and champion ourselves compared with how we support and champion the people we love.

Using either a notepad and pen, phone or laptop, write down the name of someone in your life for whom you want nothing but the best – someone you really love. Now, imagine they've come to you, completely demotivated, saying that they've fallen off track with a plan of change that means a lot to them. Your task is to get them back on track immediately. Under their name, write down all the things you'd say to ensure that they feel positive and motivated enough to push through and achieve their most meaningful goals.

Once you're finished, cross out (or delete) the name of the person you chose, and replace it with your own.

The next time you practise tuning in to your internal dialogue, if you notice that the tone you're taking with yourself is harsher than the one you'd take with someone you love, look at this list and remember that, by your own admission, these are the things people need to hear to achieve their goals. Read them; say them aloud if you can.

Over time, notice how speaking to yourself like someone you want the best for not only feels better, it enables you to choose new behaviours more easily.

Trusting yourself more than your plan

Finally, when plans don't go to plan, and you're unclear as to what the next 'kindest' move should be in the moment, ask yourself the following questions

- What would I tell someone I love to do?
- What would someone who wants the best for me tell me to do?
- What choice will I be glad I made tomorrow?

You've got this.

recipes

breakfast

slow-baked creamy berry and coconut oats

These slow baked oats feel like a combination of the creamiest bowl of porridge you've ever had and a delicious rice pudding, with hints of coconut, vanilla, maple and berries. You can mix up the fruit across the year: grated apple, chunks of pear or slices of bananas are all great additions.

Serves 4

200g jumbo oats

50g desiccated coconut

900ml plant milk (oat, almond or coconut)

200g frozen berries

6 tbsp maple syrup, plus extra to serve

2 tsp vanilla bean paste

coconut yoghurt, to serve

handful of chopped nuts (I like hazelnuts) or nut butter, to serve

1. Preheat the oven to 160°C fan.

2. Put the oats, desiccated coconut, milk, berries, maple syrup and vanilla paste into a large bowl and mix well.

3. Pour into a baking dish, approximately 25 × 20 × 6cm, smoothing the top, and bake for 45 minutes, until it has a slight wobble and you can see milk still bubbling away around the sides.

4. Remove from the oven, mix again and leave to stand for 5 minutes before serving in bowls topped with some coconut yoghurt, a drizzle of maple syrup and some chopped nuts or a drizzle of nut butter.

fruit compotes

I tend to make one of these compotes most weeks. We eat them with yoghurt and granola, use them as a topping for porridge or spoon them over our pancakes.

Each makes a small bowl, to serve 4–6

Pear, date and ginger compote

4 ripe pears, peeled, cored and roughly chopped

6 Medjool dates, pitted and roughly chopped

juice of 1 lemon, plus a strip of the peel

2 tbsp maple syrup

½ tsp ground ginger

½ tsp vanilla bean paste or ¼ tsp vanilla powder

6 tbsp water

Apple and cinnamon compote

4 eating apples, peeled, cored and roughly chopped

1 cooking apple, peeled, cored and roughly chopped

strip of lemon peel

6 tbsp maple syrup

1 tsp ground cinnamon

4 tbsp water

Berry and chia compote

450g frozen berries (I use strawberries and raspberries)

strip of lemon peel

5 tbsp maple syrup

2 tbsp chia seeds

1 star anise

1. Place all of the ingredients in a small saucepan, give them a good mix and bring to the boil over a medium heat. Turn down the heat down, put the lid on the pan and simmer for 10–15 minutes, until the fruit has softened. Remove the lemon peel – and the star anise from the berry compote – and mash or blend the fruit, depending on whether you like it totally smooth or not.

Tip for tinies

These compotes are great for weaning. Put them into a food processor and blend until completely smooth.

dark chocolate hazelnut spread

This is my absolute favourite spread and is so easy to make. It's deliciously rich, but if you prefer milk chocolate to dark, simply reduce the amount of cacao powder. Cacao is so good for us; full of antioxidants, polyphenols and magnesium.

Makes 1 jar (about 250g)

250g blanched, toasted hazelnuts

20–25g coconut sugar

20g raw cacao powder

¼ teaspoon of salt

1 tsp vanilla extract or powder

1. If the hazelnuts aren't already toasted, simply place them on a baking tray in an oven heated to 160°C fan for 8 minutes, or until golden, then remove and leave to cool.

2. Place the hazelnuts in a high-speed food processor and blend for 5–10 minutes, or until smooth.

3. Add the sugar, half the cacao and the salt to the processor and continue to blend until perfectly smooth and creamy, like nut butter; it always takes a minute more than you think.

4. Taste and add the rest of the cacao if you like quite a dark chocolatey hit, then blend again to combine.

Note

To make the spread taste more like milk chocolate, rather than dark, drop the cacao quantity to 10–15g. And if you want to swap the coconut sugar, swap it for a light brown or demerara sugar; don't use a liquid sweetener – adding liquid makes the spread much firmer and stiffer.

Rosie's big green smoothie

Smoothies are a wonderfully clever way to enjoy multiple fruits and vegetables in a sweet and refreshing drink. I often make this creamy green smoothie as a nourishing way to begin my day. Fortified plant milks are an ideal source of bone-strengthening calcium; peas will provide a great hit of plant protein; and dark leafy greens are some of the most nutrient-dense foods out there. I use this recipe as a base and switch it up based on what is in my fridge or fruit bowl, so get creative and personalise yours.

Serves 2

150ml water or plant milk of choice, plus extra to serve

70g frozen peas

1 ripe banana (best if peeled and sliced then frozen)

1 pear, cored and chopped

1 tbsp peanut or almond butter

1 Medjool date (2 if you prefer a sweeter taste)

2 blocks of frozen spinach (or 2 handfuls of fresh)

1 tbsp ground linseed

small handful of ice cubes, optional

1. Place all the ingredients in a blender and blend until smooth – it takes a few minutes to break down all the pea fibre, so keep going until it is nice and creamy. Add extra water or plant milk if needed to reach your preferred consistency.

Tip for tinies

Smoothies are a great way to add lots of fruit and veg to mealtimes.

supercharged date and banana pancakes

The protein from the hemp and chia seeds make these pancakes really filling and satisfying, while the banana and dates keeps them naturally sweet.

Serves 4

3 ripe bananas (about 300g – you want them to be very ripe, dark and spotty), chopped

grated zest of 1 lemon

4 Medjool dates, pitted and roughly chopped

2 tbsp shelled hemp seeds

1 tbsp chia seeds

185ml plant milk

150g self-raising flour

coconut oil, for frying

To serve

any of the compote recipes from page 76

berries

coconut yoghurt

shelled hemp seeds or chopped nuts

maple syrup

1. Place the bananas, lemon zest, dates, hemp seeds, chia seeds and plant milk in a food processor and blitz on a high speed for a couple of minutes until well combined and there are no lumps.

2. Add the flour and blitz again until you have a thick batter.

3. Heat a little coconut oil in a non-stick frying pan over a medium heat and fry large spoonfuls of the batter for a couple of minutes on each side. You will need to spread the mixture out a little to make 8–10cm pancakes.

4. Keep the cooked pancakes warm (under a tea towel) while you use up the remaining batter.

5. Serve the pancakes with your choice of compote or berries, some coconut yoghurt, more hemp seeds or chopped nuts and a drizzle of maple syrup.

Note
If you can't find shelled hemp seeds, they can be replaced with the equivalent measure of crunchy peanut butter.

vanilla french toast

Serves 4

2 tsp coconut oil

2 tbsp maple syrup

2 tbsp gram flour

2 tbsp ground almonds

200ml almond milk

½ tsp cinnamon

1 tsp vanilla bean paste

8 slices of bread (preferably a little stale; see tip)

For the whipped yoghurt

200g coconut yoghurt (this needs to be over 20% fat)

1 tsp coconut sugar (optional)

1 tsp vanilla bean paste

For the blueberries

150g blueberries

1 tsp maple syrup, plus extra to serve

1. First, make the whipped yoghurt. Whisk the coconut yoghurt using a stand mixer or an electric hand whisk until it becomes really thick, it will take 5–10 minutes. Once it's nice and thick and can hold its shape, add the coconut sugar, if using, and vanilla paste and whisk again for another minute. Leave to one side.

2. Place the blueberries in a large frying pan on a medium heat with a teaspoon of water and let them cook until they start to burst and release their juices, it will take about 3 minutes. Stir in the maple syrup and cook for another minute or so, until they're getting nice and juicy. Pour the blueberries and blueberry juice into a small bowl and leave to one side.

3. Next, make the French toast batter. Simply melt a teaspoon of the coconut oil, then add the melted oil plus all the remaining ingredients, except the bread, to a high-speed blender and blend for a few seconds, until smooth. You can stir the mixture together in a bowl, but I find it makes a smoother batter by quickly blending it.

4. Pour the batter into a bowl and dip the bread into it, letting it soak for 30 seconds or so and ensuring it's fully coated.

5. Wipe out the frying pan, just so the French toast doesn't go purple, then add the remaining teaspoon of coconut oil and place it over a low to medium heat. Once the oil has melted, turn the heat up to medium–high and fry the bread on each side, until golden, about 2–3 minutes. Serve with the blueberries, yoghurt and a drizzle of maple syrup.

Tip

If the bread is soft, lightly toast it, and if you're using sourdough with tough crusts, remove them.

baked beans

With maple syrup, paprika, rosemary, mustard, tamari and red wine vinegar, these are rich in flavour and brilliantly versatile. A great brunch addition, they are equally delicious as a family dinner, piled into baked sweet potatoes and served with a simple green salad drizzled with our creamy tahini dressing (see page 98).

Serves 4

1 onion, roughly chopped

1 garlic clove, roughly chopped

1 tbsp olive oil, plus extra to serve

1 tsp rosemary needles, finely chopped, or 1 tsp dried rosemary

1 tbsp tomato purée

2 tsp smoked paprika (sweet or hot)

1 tbsp maple syrup

2 tbsp tamari or soy sauce

1 tsp English mustard powder

1 × 400g tin of finely chopped tomatoes or passata

2 × 400g tins of beans (cannellini, borlotti, butter, pinto)

2 tsp red wine vinegar

sea salt and black pepper

sourdough toast, to serve

1. Preheat the oven to 160°C fan.

2. Put the onion and garlic into a food processor and blitz to a purée.

3. Heat the olive oil in an ovenproof casserole and cook the purée for 5–7 minutes until soft. Stir in the rosemary, tomato purée, paprika, maple syrup, tamari and mustard powder. Cook for another minute or so then add the chopped tomatoes and beans. Bring to a boil and transfer to the oven. Bake for 25 minutes, until the sauce has thickened slightly.

4. Remove from the oven and stir in the red wine vinegar and taste to check seasoning. Serve over sourdough toast and drizzle with a little olive oil.

Tip for tinies

Remove the tamari/soy sauce and mustard from step three, adding them at the end for the adults.

simple hash browns

These are perfect for long brunches served with our super creamy cashew and tofu scramble (see page 90), slices of avocado, sourdough and homemade baked beans (see page 86); or as a simple mid-week dinner with our black beans (see page 215), harissa chickpeas (see page 200) or garlicky salsa verde greens (see page 199).

Serves 4 (makes 16 small hash browns)

1 medium baking potato (around 470g)

1 white onion

8 tbsp gram flour

8 tbsp oat milk

1 tsp fine sea salt

black pepper

olive oil, for frying

1. Coarsely grate the potato and onion.

2. Place in a clean tea towel over a bowl and squeeze to remove as much liquid as possible.

3. Place the gram flour, oat milk, salt and some pepper in a bowl and whisk until there are no lumps. Add the grated onion and potato and stir until all of the veg has been coated in batter.

4. Heat a small drizzle of oil in a non-stick frying pan over a medium–high heat. Once it is hot and shimmering add heaped tablespoons of the mixture, flattening it out slightly as you spoon it in to ensure even cooking. Cook for 3 minutes on each side, transferring the hash browns to a baking tray as you cook each batch. (To keep them hot you can place the tray in an oven heated to 100°C fan).

Note

The potatoes will oxidise if the hash browns are left uncooked for a few hours so if you wish to make these in advance, I recommend cooking them completely and then reheating in the oven before serving.

super creamy cashew and tofu scramble

You may have tried tofu scramble before and are wondering what's special about this one. All I can say is please try it, the addition of the cashew cream and oat milk make the world of difference, making it surprisingly, almost uncannily, 'eggy'. As with the hash browns (see page 89) and baked beans (see page 86), it's great for breakfast/brunch but equally delicious as a mid-week supper.

Serves 2 as a main, 4 as part of a brunch

1 × 300g block medium firm tofu

1 tbsp tahini

2 tbsp smooth cashew cream (see page 107)

6 tbsp oat milk

½ tsp ground turmeric

⅛ teaspoon smoked paprika

½ teaspoon sea salt

black pepper

1 garlic clove, finely chopped

olive oil, for frying

1. Pat the tofu dry with a piece of kitchen paper. Tear it into bite-size chunks using your hands, they don't need to be too small as they will break down further during cooking.

2. In a medium bowl whisk together all the other ingredients, except the olive oil, until smooth and set aside.

3. Heat a drizzle of olive oil in a non-stick frying pan over medium-high heat. Add the tofu pieces and cook until golden, about 5–6 minutes. Resist the temptation to turn them too much during cooking as this will prevent them from turning golden brown, but do flip them to ensure each side takes on some colour. You can also break the tofu down into smaller pieces, depending on whether you like your tofu scramble loose or chunky.

4. When the tofu is golden pour in the liquid mixture and stir over the heat until all is smooth, glossy and piping hot, about 2–3 minutes. Serve immediately.

making
life
simpler

crispy chickpeas

A great alternative to crisps and they can be stored in an airtight container for a couple of days if they last long enough!

Serves 4

2 × 400g tins of chickpeas, drained

2 tbsp olive oil

2 tsp ground cumin

2 tsp sea salt

2 tsp dried chipotle flakes or 1 tsp dried chilli flakes

½ tsp dried or fresh rosemary needles (finely chopped if using fresh)

1. Preheat the oven to 180°C fan. Line a baking tray with baking paper.

2. Mix everything together in a large bowl then spread the chickpeas out evenly in the tray.

3. Bake in the oven for 40 minutes, stirring halfway through.

4. Remove from the oven, leave to cool for a few minutes then serve.

herby dressing

This dressing instantly adds colour and flavour to the simplest meal. It's perfect with tray bakes, root veggie salads and is great for livening up leftovers.

140g cashews

150ml almond milk

20g fresh parsley

20g fresh coriander

juice of 2 limes

4 tbsp olive oil

1 garlic clove

2 tsp maple syrup

generous pinch of sea salt

1. Place the cashews in a bowl, cover with boiling water and let them soak for 5–10 minutes. If you're short on time just 5 minutes is enough (so long as you have a good blender), but the longer they soak the smoother the dressing.

2. Drain the cashews and place them in a blender with the remaining ingredients. Blitz until smooth and creamy, adding a splash of water if needed. Season to taste.

Note

To make a herby kale salad like the one in the photo opposite, put several handfuls of kale into a bowl and massage with the herby dressing for 2–3 minutes, until soft, then top with the crispy chickpeas.

walnut parmesan

This nutty 'parmesan' is an easy way to add extra flavour and nutrients into your day – it's really quick to make and lasts for ages, so we always have some in our fridge. Walnuts are a great source of omega-3 fatty acids, which is something many of us don't eat enough of, but this makes it really easy to get your daily dose. I sprinkle this on to all our pasta dishes, as well as tray bakes, risottos and grains.

Makes about 200g

100g walnuts

100g macadamia or cashew nuts

20g nutritional yeast

⅓ teaspoon garlic powder

⅓ teaspoon sea salt

1. Preheat the oven to 170°C fan.

2. Place the nuts on a baking sheet and toast them in the hot oven for 5 minutes, then leave to cool.

3. Once cool, simply add all the ingredients to a food processor and pulse for 30 seconds or so, until you have a fine meal. Store in the fridge for up to two weeks.

Note

This works really well sprinkled on top of pasta served with any of the pesto recipes on page 112.

Tip for tinies

A sprinkle of this is a great way to up the nutritional content of a speedy pasta dinner.

97

creamy tahini dressing

I eat a lot of simple, leftover salad bowls during the week with a mix of grains, roasted root veggies, fresh greens and beans or chickpeas. When I need a dressing to bring it all together, this is what I use.

Makes a small bowl, about 150ml

2 garlic cloves, crushed

juice of 1 lemon

4 tbsp tahini

2 tsp maple syrup

sea salt

1. In a mixing bowl, combine the garlic and lemon juice. Whisk in the tahini – it will become thicker and lighter in colour. Add 3–4 tablespoons of water and continue to mix until you have a pourable consistency. Add the maple syrup and season to taste.

2. Transfer the dressing to a jar, cover and keep in the fridge for up to three days.

crunchy croutons

Homemade croutons are so easy to prepare, but they really bring a simple dish to life by adding a lovely crunch, plus they're a great way to use up leftover bread. I use these croutons to top the everyday minestrone and golden sweet potato and lentil soup and in the everyday salad (see pages 166, 163 and 221).

Makes 200g

200g sourdough bread (best made with bread that's a few days old), cut into 2cm chunks

6 tbsp extra virgin olive oil

1 garlic clove, finely sliced

1 tsp sea salt

1 tbsp nutritional yeast (optional)

1. Preheat the oven to 180°C fan. Mix together the bread chunks, oil, garlic and salt, plus the nutritional yeast if you're using it, so the bread is covered in the oil. Spread the cubes out on a baking tray and bake in the oven for 8–10 minutes until golden. Leave to cool, then store in an airtight container for up to a week.

Notes

Some tahini brands are denser and more bitter than others so look for one that's very smooth and creamy. To throw together a really quick avo, tahini and chickpea salad (see photo, opposite), toss together some salad leaves, chunks of avocado, the crispy chickpeas from page 94 and the croutons then drizzle over the creamy tahini dressing and add some chopped chives.

dukkah

My kitchen is always stocked with big batches of soups, sauces, and add-ons, like this dukkah. It's a mixture of nuts, seeds and spices – originally from Egypt – and is just such an easy way to add a huge amount of flavour to a simple recipe. Try it sprinkled over the black beans on toast on page 215, and with the coconut rice on page 142.

Makes 1 jar (300g)

100g sesame seeds

50g salted peanuts

50g walnuts

50g sunflower seeds

50g pumpkin seeds

1 tbsp coriander seeds

1 tbsp fennel seeds

½ tbsp cumin seeds

2 tsp sea salt

1. Heat a large frying pan over a medium heat and toast all of the ingredients together for 5–10 minutes, stirring frequently.

2. Once the sesame seeds have turned golden (they are your guide so watch they don't burn) remove the pan from the heat and transfer the mixture to a food processor.

3. Pulse for a couple of minutes until roughly chopped and, once cool, store in an airtight container for up to two weeks.

salsa verde

This versatile sauce will add tang and depth to a wealth of dishes.
I recommend trying it with our easy root veg tray bake (see page 185),
with lots of greens in a baked jacket potato (see page 199) or with
our courgette or carrot fritters (see pages 150 and 153).

Makes about 200g

2 garlic cloves, peeled

25g parsley

25g mint

25g basil

1 tbsp Dijon mustard

2 tbsp capers, drained and roughly chopped

2 tbsp apple cider vinegar

120ml olive oil

sea salt and black pepper

1. Finely chop the garlic, along with the herbs. Place in a mixing bowl and add the mustard, capers and vinegar.

2. Slowly pour in the oil, stirring all the time, until you have a spoonable sauce. Season to taste.

3. Transfer to a jar and keep in the fridge for 2–3 days.

harissa

Harissa is an amazing, aromatic North African paste, which I add to everything from dips to dressings, tray bakes, soups and stews. It's an easy way to instantly liven up any meal. It is traditionally made with dried guajillo chillies, but these aren't easy to find in mainstream supermarkets, so we've skipped them in this recipe.

Makes 125–150ml

2 tsp coriander seeds (or swap for ground coriander if you don't have a pestle and mortar)

2 tsp cumin seeds (or ground cumin)

1 tsp sweet smoked paprika

4 garlic cloves, peeled and chopped

4 red chillies, halved and deseeded

juice of ½ lemon, or to taste

75ml olive oil , plus extra for storing

sea salt and black pepper

1. Toast the coriander, cumin seeds and paprika in a dry frying pan for 1–2 minutes, until fragrant.

2. Grind the spices in a pestle and mortar, then purée with the remaining ingredients in a blender until fine. Season and add more lemon juice, to taste.

3. Transfer the paste to a jar, cover with a little oil and refrigerate. The paste will keep in the fridge for two to three weeks.

Notes

Harissa should have a spicy kick, but you can tone it down to make it more family friendly. Just swap the chillies for half a red pepper. I add harissa to the cauliflower and cashew pilaf tray bake on page 174 and the piri piri tray bake on page 177.

smooth cashew cream

This is a staple in our house. It's so light and brilliant to have on hand for a variety of dishes – basically whenever you need something to replace dairy cream, this is your go-to. I use it in everything from a super simple pasta sauce – just add spaghetti, peas and sautéed spinach – to our one-tray nachos (see page 182), fajitas (see page 237) or a speedy BLT (see page 209).

Makes 1 bowl (about 400g)

250g raw, unsalted cashews

125ml water or unsweetened almond milk

4 tbsp olive oil

1 tbsp nutritional yeast

½ tbsp maple syrup

2 plump garlic cloves, crushed

large pinch of sea salt

lemon juice, to taste

1. Place the cashews in a mixing bowl, cover with boiling water and let them soak for 5–10 minutes. If you're short on time just 5 minutes is enough (so long as you have a good blender), but the longer they soak the smoother the sauce. If you're very organised, leave them in the fridge to soak overnight.

2. Once the cashews are soft, drain them, discarding the soaking water. Place them in a high-speed blender with the remaining ingredients and blend until smooth and creamy.

3. Transfer to an airtight container and store in the fridge. Use within three days.

Note
I like adding a teaspoon of Dijon mustard to this sometimes – it's great for a little more depth, but it's less popular with our girls.

cucumber and mint raita

This cooling yoghurt-based dip is the perfect accompaniment to any spiced dish. Try it with the moong dhal on page 154 and the chana bateta on page 157.

Makes 1 bowl

⅓ cucumber

150g coconut yoghurt

2 tbsp fresh mint, finely chopped

½ teaspoon fine sea salt

1 teaspoon olive oil

1. Slice the cucumber in half and scrape out the seeds and pulp. Coarsley grate and place in a medium bowl.

2. Add the remaining ingredients and stir to combine.

chermoula

Makes 1 medium bowl

2 tsp smoked paprika

2 tsp ground cumin

25g coriander

25g parsley

4 garlic cloves, roughly chopped

juice of 1 lemon

1 red chilli, halved, deseeded and roughly chopped (optional)

4 tbsp olive oil, plus extra for storing

1. Toast the smoked paprika and cumin in a dry frying pan for 1–2 minutes, until fragrant. Remove and set aside to cool.

2. Put the cooled spices into a blender with the coriander, parsley, garlic, lemon juice and chilli, if using. Gradually add the olive oil and blend to a rough paste.

3. Transfer the paste to a jar, cover with a little oil and refrigerate. The paste will keep in the fridge for 3–4 days.

our go-to pestos

Pesto is a staple in our house, as it's just such a quick way to bring a meal together. It seems to be the one meal everyone will always eat. I have a jar in my fridge at all times and we use it at least a few times a week, which is why I like to mix up what goes into it. I have shared our classic basil pesto too – I use this in everything from our mushroom, lentil and pesto wheels on page 259 to the courgette and herb fritters on page 153.

Each pesto serves 4

Rocket and pistachio pesto

60g shelled pistachios

2 garlic cloves, roughly chopped

100g rocket leaves, roughly chopped

100ml extra virgin olive oil , plus extra for the jar

3 tbsp nutritional yeast

juice of ½ lemon

Almond and tomato pesto

60g whole almonds

2 garlic cloves, roughly chopped

100g basil, large stems discarded, leaves roughly shredded

100ml extra virgin olive oil , plus extra for the jar

8 sun-dried tomatoes in oil, drained and roughly chopped

2 tbsp nutritional yeast

juice of ½ lemon

Basil pesto

60g pine nuts

2 garlic cloves, peeled and roughly chopped

100g basil, large stems discarded, leaves roughly shredded

100ml extra virgin olive oil, plus extra for the jar

3 tbsp nutritional yeast

juice of ½ lemon

1. Toast the nuts in a small frying pan over a gentle heat for 2–3 minutes, until golden. Remove from the heat and set aside to cool.

2. Blend the nuts with the garlic, herb or rocket, and the olive oil (and the sun-dried tomatoes for the almond pesto). Add the nutritional yeast and season with lemon juice, to taste.

3. Transfer the pesto to a jar, pour over a layer of olive oil and cover. The pesto will keep in the fridge for up to a week.

roasted walnut and red pepper dip

This chapter is filled with the recipes I fill my fridge with, the ones that make busy weeks so much easier, and this is no exception. It's lovely and rich and works beautifully in recipes like the root veg and pickled red onion tart on page 195.

Makes 1 bowl (about 400g)

2 red peppers

150g walnuts

2 garlic cloves, peeled and left whole

80ml extra virgin olive oil

2 tbsp red wine vinegar

sea salt and black pepper

1. Preheat the oven to 180°C fan.

2. Place the peppers on a baking tray and roast in the oven for 20 minutes, then add the walnuts and garlic cloves and return to the oven for 10 minutes.

3. Remove from the oven, transfer the peppers to a bowl and cover with a tea towel. Leave them to steam for 5 minutes – this will make the skins easier to peel off.

4. Remove the skins, seeds and stalks from the peppers and place the flesh into a food processor along with the walnuts, garlic, oil and vinegar. Season with salt and black pepper.

5. Blitz on a high speed until you have a dip consistency; add a splash of water if you like it a little runnier.

minty pea dip

We've eaten this almost every week since I can remember. It's my go-to when I'm short on time and creativity. I'll roast a simple tray of veg and serve this on the side. The leftovers then make a great dip later in the week. It's so quick to make and incredibly versatile. Plus, it's really nutritious; peas are loaded with protein, fibre, vitamins and minerals.

Makes 1 bowl (about 400g)

250g frozen peas

100g cashews

2 tbsp mint leaves, finely chopped

2 tbsp extra virgin olive oil

splash of oat milk

½ lime

sea salt and black pepper

1. Put the peas and cashews into a bowl and cover with boiling water. Set aside to soak for 5 minutes.

2. Drain the peas and cashews then transfer to a blender along with the remaining ingredients, seasoning to taste. Blitz on a high speed for a couple of minutes until you have a smooth purée.

Note

I use a blender to make the dip because it makes it smoother, but you can also use a food processor.

lemon and almond
butter hummus

The mix of roasted garlic, almond butter and lemon zest does
absolute wonders for this twist on a classic hummus. It's zestier and fresher,
and makes the perfect filling for a speedy pitta or veggie wrap.

Makes 1 bowl (about 350g)

1 × 400g tin of chickpeas, drained but
reserve 3 tablespoons of the liquid

1 large clove of roasted garlic (see page
115), peeled and roughly chopped

1 tbsp almond butter

finely grated zest and juice of ½ lemon

60ml extra virgin olive oil

sea salt and black pepper

1. Place all of the ingredients in a blender, including the reserved chickpea liquid, and
blitz on a high speed until smooth, adding a splash more olive oil or water as needed
to get the consistency you like. Season to taste.

Note

You really don't miss the tahini in this – the lemon zest and garlic more than make up
for it. To ring the changes you could swap a teaspoon or so of black garlic paste for
the garlic clove or add 1 tablespoon of finely chopped herbs.

Tip for tinies

Skip the lemon zest if the flavour is a bit zingy for your little ones.

herby butter bean dip

Herby, creamy, zesty and so easy to make, this will quickly become a staple in your house. It's a great one to batch cook on a Sunday night for adding to sandwiches, wraps, grain bowls or roast veggies during the week.

Makes 1 bowl (about 350g)

100ml extra virgin olive oil

2 rosemary sprigs, leaves stripped and finely chopped

2 garlic cloves, finely sliced

½ tsp thyme leaves

small bunch of flat-leaf parsley, roughly chopped

1 × 400g tin of butterbeans, drained and rinsed

finely grated zest of 1 lemon

squeeze of lemon juice, to taste

sea salt and black pepper

1. Heat the olive oil, rosemary, garlic and thyme leaves over a gentle heat for a couple of minutes and set aside to infuse for a couple of minutes.

2. Put the parsley, butter beans, lemon zest and juice, salt and pepper and a splash of water into a food processor and blitz for a couple of minutes on a high speed.

3. Pour in the infused oil along with the herbs and garlic and blitz again until you have a smooth purée.

4. Add a splash more water if you prefer it a little runnier.

Note

This is lovely on toast for a very speedy lunch, or it would work brilliantly as a canapé spread on top of crostini with some of the crispy chickpeas from page 94 or dukkah from page 101.

Tip for tinies

My girls love this; it's been a really easy way to get lots of nutrients into quick post-nursery lunches. I just spread it on toast or they dip rice cakes into it.

golden paste and an easy broth

Whenever I feel run down or one of us is ill, I make this and it hits the spot every time. It's absolutely loaded with anti-inflammatory ingredients and each sip truly feels equal parts delicious and intensely nourishing. I use the paste in a few other recipes – with noodles, in a curry and in a sweet potato soup (see pages 161, 158 and 163). One paste, 10 minutes to make it; four delicious recipes.

Serves 4

For the golden paste

2 shallots

40g ginger

5 garlic cloves

3 Thai red chillies

2 tsp ground turmeric

1 tsp ground coriander

1 tsp ground cumin

1 tsp ground paprika

3 tsp sesame oil

juice of 1 lime

For the broth

1 tbsp sesame oil

1 shallot (you can use onions, but shallots give it a sweeter, more subtle flavour), finely sliced

4 garlic cloves, finely sliced

500ml boiling water

2 × 400ml tins of coconut milk

1 tsp coconut sugar

sea salt

lime wedges, to serve

1. To make the paste, simply peel the shallots, ginger and garlic, then place all of the ingredients in a food processor and whizz until a paste forms. Store the paste in an airtight container in the fridge for up to 2 weeks.

2. To make the broth, pour the sesame oil into a saucepan that has a lid. Place over a medium heat, add the shallot, fry for 2 minutes or so, then add the garlic and a sprinkling of salt. Let this cook for a further 5 minutes, until soft.

3. Add 5 tablespoons of the golden paste and cook for another 2 minutes.

4. Add the boiling water, this will clean the bottom of the pan and absorb all those flavours, then add the coconut milk and coconut sugar.

5. Bring to the boil, then place the lid on the pan and let it simmer on a low heat for 45 minutes to 1 hour – the longer it cooks the deeper the flavour will be. Pour into large mugs or bowls, add a squeeze of lime and salt to taste.

Tip for tinies

Remove the chillies from the paste if you're cooking for younger children. I like to add a sprinkling of chilli flakes at the end for the adult portions.

from the
hob

garlicky roasted aubergine ragu

This was the first recipe I created for the book, and it's still a real favourite.
May absolutely loves it and gobbles it up, before shouting 'more, more'.
It's great for batch cooking and is delicious with spaghetti, orzo, piled on
to a jacket potato, or you can serve it with whichever grain you have
in the house – quinoa (for extra protein), barley or rice.

Serves 4

2 medium aubergines

1 tbsp olive oil

1 red onion, finely sliced

1 white onion, finely sliced

5 large garlic cloves, crushed

1–2 tsp smoked paprika

2 tsp maple syrup

1 × 400g tin of brown lentils, drained
and rinsed

1 × 400g tin of chopped tomatoes

4 servings of spaghetti (75g per person)

1 tsp brown rice miso

½ tsp apple cider vinegar

sea salt and pepper

handful of fresh parsley, finely chopped,
to serve

sprinkling of walnut parmesan (see page
97), to serve

1. Heat the oven to 210°C fan.

2. Pierce the aubergines all over with a knife – this allows them to release steam as
they cook – then place them on a baking tray and roast for about an hour, until the
skin blisters and gently chars, while the inside cooks slowly. Once they're cooked, the
skin will be wrinkled and shrivelled, and it'll look as though they've collapsed.

3. After they've been in the oven for about 30 minutes, start to make the ragu.

4. Put a large frying pan over a medium heat and add the olive oil, a generous
sprinkling of salt and the onions. After 5 minutes, once the onions start to soften, add
the garlic. Let this cook for another 2–3 minutes.

5. Add the paprika, letting it cook for 2 minutes or so, before adding the maple syrup,
stir, then add the lentils. Mix well and a few minutes later add the chopped tomatoes.

6. Once the aubergines have cooked, slice them open and scoop the flesh out with a
spoon – it should be silky smooth.

7. Mash the aubergine into the lentil mixture and let the mixture simmer for a further
10 minutes. Meanwhile, cook the spaghetti according to the instructions on the pack.

8. Finally add the miso and apple cider vinegar to the ragu and taste to check the
seasoning. Toss the pasta into the pan of ragu and mix well. Serve each portion
sprinkled with fresh parsley and some walnut parmesan.

one-pan veggie and butter bean orzo

A simple, midweek dinner that loads you up on veggies and plant protein. The coconut milk makes it deliciously creamy, and the leftovers make for a brilliant speedy lunch later in the week – reheat it gently over a low heat with a drizzle of olive oil.

Serves 4

1 tbsp olive oil

1 white onion, diced

1 small red onion, diced

3 garlic cloves, crushed

1 sweet pointed pepper, diced

1 tsp smoked paprika

1 × 400g tin of butter beans, drained and rinsed

300g orzo

400ml vegetable stock

1 × 400ml tin of coconut milk

100g frozen peas

200g cherry tomatoes, quartered

20g fresh basil, finely chopped

juice of ½ lemon

salt and pepper

1. Place a large saucepan on a medium heat and add the olive oil and a generous sprinkling of salt. Once it's warm add the onions and cook for 5 minutes, until softened.

2. Add the garlic and pepper and cook for a further 5 minutes, until the pepper starts to soften.

3. Add the paprika and butter beans, cook for a minute or so before adding the orzo, stock and coconut milk. Bring to the boil, then turn the heat down to low, place the lid on the pan and simmer for 15 minutes stirring it every 5 minutes or so.

4. Add the peas and cherry tomatoes, stirring them through. Cook everything for a further 5 minutes, until the tomatoes soften and the peas are cooked. Then stir through the basil and lemon juice and season to taste.

Tip for tinies
Cut the butter beans in half for very little ones.

super greens pasta

As soon as cavolo nero comes into season I add it to our weekly meal plan. It's the easiest, most delicious way to load up on greens. I hold off on the chilli when I make this for the girls, but it adds delicious depth if you like a little heat.

Serves 4

1 tbsp olive oil, plus extra to serve

2 shallots (or swap for onions)

6 garlic cloves

pinch of dried chilli flakes

400g cavolo nero

100g spinach

4 servings of spaghetti (75g per person)

sea salt

For the sauce

75g pine nuts

juice of 1 lemon

2 tbsp coconut yoghurt

2 tbsp pasta water

2 tbsp olive oil

20g basil

20g parsley

1. Toast the pine nuts in a large frying pan over a medium heat for about 3 minutes – you want them to go nice and golden. Remove them from the pan and leave to one side (you'll use the same pan to cook the greens).

2. Place the pan back on a medium heat, add a glug of olive oil and a sprinkling of salt, then, once the pan is warm, fry the shallots, letting them cook for 5–10 minutes before adding the garlic and chilli.

3. While they cook, either finely slice or quickly blitz (in a food processor) the cavolo nero and spinach until they're very finely shredded, and add them to the pan.

4. Meanwhile, cook the pasta in boiling salted water according to the instructions on the pack.

5. Place the sauce ingredients in a food processor or blender and pulse until smooth (you'll need to wait until the pasta is almost ready before adding 2 tablespoons of the pasta water to the blender).

6. Drain the pasta, reserving a little of the water, and add the pasta to the pan with the greens and the sauce. Toss until the sauce coats the pasta, adding the reserved pasta water to loosen if needed. Add a generous glug of olive oil to finish, then serve immediately.

creamy beetroot and walnut spaghetti

The most vibrant dish in the book, this bright pink spaghetti is a real winner. The mix of walnuts, pine nuts and white beans gives it a lovely texture, the coconut milk makes it beautifully creamy. The beets bring the colour and the garlic and parsley really add to the flavour. The result is sweet and mild, almost like a korma sauce.

Serves 4

100g walnuts

50g pine nuts

300g cooked beetroot, drained, peeled and roughly chopped

25g flat-leaf parsley, roughly chopped

3 tbsp olive oil

1 red onion, finely sliced

1 garlic clove, finely sliced

1 × 400g tin of small white beans (cannellini or haricot), drained

200ml tinned coconut milk, shaken well to disperse the cream

lemon juice, to taste

4 servings of spaghetti or other long pasta (75g per person)

sea salt and black pepper

1. Toast the walnuts and pine nuts in a dry frying pan over a high heat until the pine nuts are golden, then transfer to a food processor along with the beetroot, parsley, 2 tablespoons of the olive oil and a good pinch of salt. Blitz until you have a thick purée.

2. Heat the remaining tablespoon of olive oil in a large casserole and fry the onion for 5–7 minutes, until soft. Stir in the garlic and fry for another minute.

3. Transfer the beetroot purée to the pan along with the beans and coconut milk and mix everything together. Bring to the boil and simmer for a couple of minutes to heat everything through.

4. Check the seasoning then stir in lemon juice to taste.

5. Cook the spaghetti according to the instructions on the pack, then drain well and return to the pan.

6. Stir the sauce through the pasta and serve immediately.

roasted squash and crispy sage pappardelle

A beautifully creamy, smooth sauce tossed with pappardelle and topped with crispy fried sage and fragrant slices of garlic. It's relatively easy to make too, simply slow-roast the squash, pan-fry the sage and garlic with lots of olive oil, wilt the spinach and bring it all together.

Serves 4

1 large squash (butternut, crown prince, onion), about 1kg

2 tbsp olive oil

1 small onion, peeled and quartered

4 garlic cloves, peeled

50ml extra virgin olive oil

small handful of sage leaves

25ml oat milk

150g baby spinach, roughly chopped

nutmeg, to taste (no more than ½ tsp)

4 servings of pappardelle or tagliatelle (75g per person)

sea salt and black pepper

1. Preheat the oven to 190°C fan.

2. Cut the squash in half and scoop out the seeds. Season the flesh with some salt and drizzle with the 2 tablespoons of oil then place cut side down in a baking tray along with the onion quarters. Tuck two garlic cloves inside the cavity of the squash and roast for 45–50 minutes, or until the skin is blistered and the flesh is soft.

3. Slice the remaining garlic cloves finely then gently heat the extra virgin olive oil in a large frying pan and fry the garlic and sage leaves for a couple of minutes, until the garlic is golden and the leaves are crisp. Remove the garlic and sage with a slotted spoon and set aside, reserving the oil in the pan.

4. When the squash is cooked, scoop out the flesh and place it in a blender or food processor along with the roasted onions, garlic and oat milk. Season well with salt and pepper and blitz to a smooth purée.

5. Transfer the purée to the oil in the frying pan and stir to combine. Add the spinach, grate in some nutmeg to taste, and cook until the spinach has wilted and the sauce is bubbling.

6. Cook the pasta according to the instructions on the pack. Drain and toss with the sauce, then scatter over the fried garlic and sage leaves.

Tip for tinies

Without the nutmeg (or just a little less) and crispy sage leaves, this is fantastic for little ones.

broccoli, pistachio and chilli pasta

A simple, speedy recipe with a lovely balance of spice, zest and freshness. Delicious with al dente pasta, orzo or jacket potatoes.

Serves 4

4 servings of short pasta, such as fusilli, orecchiette or casarecce (75g per person)

1 large head of broccoli (600g), stalk finely chopped and florets roughly chopped (1–2cm)

2 tbsp extra virgin olive oil, plus extra to serve

2 large garlic cloves, peeled and finely sliced

1 red chilli, deseeded and finely sliced (optional)

50g pistachios, shelled and finely chopped

grated zest of ½ lemon

20g parsley, leaves and stalks finely chopped

sea salt and black pepper

1. Cook the pasta according to the instructions on the pack.

2. Add the broccoli florets and stalks to a saucepan of salted boiling water and simmer for 3 minutes – you want them to be almost fully cooked but not soft.

3. Drain the broccoli, keeping back a few tablespoons of the cooking water, and set aside.

4. Heat the olive oil in a large frying pan and add the sliced garlic and chilli (if using), fry for a couple of minutes then stir in the pistachios and lemon zest and remove from the heat.

5. Transfer the broccoli to the frying pan. Season well then put the pan back on the heat and add a couple of tablespoons of the broccoli cooking water.

6. Fry everything for a couple of minutes, squashing the broccoli as you go, then stir in the chopped parsley.

7. Stir through the pasta with a generous drizzle of olive oil.

Tip for tinies

For little children, simply leave out the chilli. You can also blitz the sauce in a food processor or blender with some more broccoli cooking water or oat milk to make a smoother, thicker sauce if this one is too chunky.

one-pot mediterranean pasta

Everyone needs a go-to roster of one-pot meals, they're a life saver on busy days when you need a delicious meal without all the washing up that normally goes with it. The capers, olives, chilli, parsley and vinegar make this recipe perfectly punchy, and even better it comes together in just 20 minutes.

Serves 4

2 tbsp olive oil

4 garlic cloves, finely sliced

2 tbsp capers, rinsed and patted dry

handful of pitted Kalamata olives, quartered

1 red, orange or yellow pepper, finely sliced

1 tsp dried chilli flakes

8 sun-dried tomatoes, finely chopped

20g parsley, stalks and leaves separated and finely chopped

2 tbsp tomato purée

2 tbsp balsamic vinegar

1 × 400g tin of chopped tomatoes

550ml water

4 servings of farfalle, conchiglie or penne (75g per person)

1. Heat the oil in a large casserole and cook the garlic, capers, olives, pepper, chilli and sun-dried tomatoes on a medium heat for 10 minutes until the peppers have softened.

2. Turn up the heat and stir in the parsley stalks, tomato purée and balsamic vinegar.

3. Cook for a couple of minutes then pour in the chopped tomatoes and water. Stir in the pasta and bring to the boil.

4. Turn down the heat, cover and simmer for 12 minutes, stirring regularly to prevent sticking.

5. Mix in the parsley leaves and serve immediately.

Tip for tinies
Skip the chillies and the olives (depending on their age), then add them at the end for the adults.

spicy peanut noodles

Serves 4

200g vermicelli rice noodles

1 × 300g block of firm tofu

olive oil, for frying

1 red onion, finely sliced

2 garlic cloves, finely chopped

thumb-sized piece of ginger, finely chopped

125g frozen peas

2 spring onions, finely sliced, to serve

For the sauce

3 tbsp tamari

2 tbsp rice wine vinegar

2 tbsp crunchy peanut butter

2 tsp maple syrup

4 tbsp water

1 tsp curry powder

½ tsp turmeric

½–1 tsp dried chili flake

For the quick pickled chillies

2 red chillies, deseeded and finely chopped

juice of 2 limes

1 tsp maple syrup

1. Cook the noodles according to the instructions on the pack. Drain, run under cold water to stop the cooking process and set aside.

2. Pat the tofu dry with a paper towel and cut it into bite-sized cubes.

3. Place all the sauce ingredients in a medium bowl and whisk until smooth. Set aside.

4. For the quick pickled chillies, place the chillies in a small bowl and pour over the lime juice and maple syrup. Set aside.

5. Heat a drizzle of olive oil in a non-stick frying pan over a medium–high heat. Once it is hot and shimmering add the tofu and cook until golden brown and crispy on all sides, about 7–8 minutes. Try not to stir it too often during cooking as that will prevent it from crisping up, but ensure that all sides get enough contact with the hot oil to turn golden.

6. Once the tofu is golden and crispy add the onion, garlic and ginger and cook until beginning to soften, 1–2 minutes. Add the frozen peas and cook for a further minute. Add the sauce and cook, stirring occasionally, for about 3 minutes, until everything is piping hot and the sauce has thickened slightly.

7. Add the noodles, using a set of tongs or two forks to toss gently over the heat. Once all the noodles are coated in the sauce, turn off the heat, pour over the quick pickled chillies and their liquid, and toss to combine. Sprinkle with the spring onion and serve immediately.

Tip for tinies

Add the pickled chilli at the end, after you've served their portions. Depending on their age, reduce or remove the tamari, and use smooth peanut butter.

coconut rice with steamed greens

A one-pan wonder and a true weeknight saviour that always hits the spot after a long day. It's simple but flavoursome, relatively quick to make and of course packed with veg. If you want to add a little more depth, try drizzling it with our herb garnish from the garlic mushrooms with butter bean mash on page 233.

Serves 4

1 tbsp coconut oil

1 small onion, finely chopped

2cm piece of ginger, grated

2 garlic cloves, grated

1 tbsp ground coriander

small bunch of coriander, stalks finely chopped, leaves reserved for garnishing

3 tbsp desiccated coconut

200g basmati rice

1 × 400g tin of coconut milk

200ml hot vegetable stock

200g green beans, halved

200g mangetout or sugar snap peas, trimmed

200g frozen peas

200g frozen edamame beans

sea salt and black pepper

2 limes, halved, to serve

dukkah (see page 101), to serve

1. Heat the coconut oil in a 28–30cm lidded casserole over a medium heat.

2. Add the onion and fry for 5 minutes until it browns a little then add the ginger, garlic, ground coriander, coriander stalks and desiccated coconut. Fry for another 2–3 minutes.

3. Add the rice and coconut milk; rinse the tin out with the stock, then add that too. Season well with salt and pepper and stir briefly to bring everything together.

4. Bring to the boil then carefully lay the vegetables on top of the rice. Put the lid on, turn the heat down as low as it can go and let everything steam for 15 minutes.

5. Remove from the heat and set aside for 5 minutes.

6. Serve the rice and greens with the lime halves. Sprinkle over the reserved coriander leaves and a generous helping of dukkah.

warm grain salad with green beans and olives

Serves 4

1 tbsp olive oil

1 fennel bulb, chopped

100g wild rice

500ml hot vegetable stock

100g brown basmati

50g quinoa

400g green beans, trimmed and cut into thirds

100g pine nuts

75g pitted green olives, roughly chopped

2 tbsp capers, rinsed and roughly chopped

250g cooked beetroot, roughly chopped

small bunch of dill, finely chopped

sea salt and black pepper

For the dressing

grated zest and juice of 1 lemon

2 tbsp Dijon mustard

2 garlic cloves, crushed or finely grated

100ml extra virgin olive oil

1. In a large, lidded casserole, heat the olive oil then add the fennel. Stir over a high heat for 5 minutes until the fennel has softened and begun to caramelise.

2. Add the wild rice and hot vegetable stock. Season with salt and pepper, stir briefly and bring to the boil. Cook for 5 minutes.

3. Add the basmati rice, stir briefly and bring back to the boil.

4. Put the lid on, turn the heat down as low as it can go and simmer for 25 minutes.

5. Add the quinoa, stirring it through the rice, then scatter the green beans over the grains, put the lid back on and cook for another 10 minutes. If you are worried about the rice burning, give it a quick stir. Once the quinoa is cooked, remove the pan from the heat and leave to steam for a further 10 minutes – the grains will soak up any remaining liquid.

6. Toast the pine nuts in a dry frying pan over a high heat then set aside. Watch them like a hawk as they burn easily!

7. Transfer the cooked grains and beans to a serving dish. Whisk the dressing ingredients together and pour over the salad, stirring together with the olives and capers. Gently fold in the beetroot (you don't want it to discolour the salad), and scatter the pine nuts and dill over the top. Serve immediately.

Notes

You can just use brown basmati for this if you can't find wild rice. You could also use red camargue rice or black rice.

easy tabbouleh-style salad with pearl barley

I love the pearl barley in this salad, it's a little chewy and gives this a great texture. It's delicious serves with our lemon and almond butter hummus (see page 118), and a big green salad. The leftovers make a great on-the-go lunch too.

Serves 4 as a main or 8 as a side

200g pearl barley

1 small cucumber (about 200g), diced

200g cherry tomatoes, quartered

2 celery sticks, finely sliced

50g mint, leaves finely chopped

50g parsley, finely chopped

½ red onion, finely chopped

seeds from 1 pomegranate

90ml extra virgin olive oil

juice of 2 lemons

1 tbsp pomegranate molasses or maple syrup

sea salt and black pepper

1. Put the pearl barley into a saucepan and cover with at least 3cm water. Season with salt, bring to the boil and simmer for 30 minutes, until tender. Top up with more water if necessary.

2. Meanwhile, in a large bowl, mix together the cucumber, tomatoes, celery, mint, parsley, red onion and half the pomegranate seeds.

3. Whisk together the olive oil, lemon juice and pomegranate molasses or maple syrup and pour over the chopped vegetables.

4. Drain the pearl barley and stir through the vegetables – the warm barley will soak up the dressing.

5. Scatter over the remaining pomegranate seeds and serve immediately.

Note

To make this in a hurry, swap barley for quinoa, which is ready in 12-15 minutes.

corn, polenta and spring onion fritters

These are a delicious speedy dinner – they come together in just 15 minutes or so. I serve them with a simple side salad tossed with our creamy tahini dressing (see page 98) or mashed avocado, hot sauce and lime wedges.

Makes 20 (to serve 4)

75g plain flour

25g polenta

1½ tsp baking powder

½ tsp fine sea salt

1 × 340g can sweetcorn, drained and patted dry

2 spring onions, finely sliced

1 garlic clove, peeled and crushed

1 red chilli, deseeded and diced

about 8 coriander sprigs, finely chopped

1 tbsp nutritional yeast

150ml oat milk

1–2 tbsp olive oil

1. In a large mixing bowl, whisk together the flour, polenta, baking powder and salt. Season well and stir through the sweetcorn, spring onions, garlic, chilli (to taste), coriander and nutritional yeast.

2. Gradually stir in the milk to create a thick, spoonable batter.

3. Wipe a large frying pan with a little of the oil and place over a medium–high heat. Once hot, add tablespoons of the mixture, spaced apart, and fry for 2–3 minutes. Once bubbles appear on the surface of the fritters and they are set at the edges, flip and cook for a further 90 seconds or so, until golden and crisp. Transfer to kitchen paper to drain.

4. Repeat with the remaining batter.

Tip for tinies

Remove the chillies and add a sprinkle of dried chilli flakes to the adult portions instead.

crispy carrot fritters

This simple fritter recipe is brilliantly versatile and full of flavour. It's ideal for lunch boxes and simple mid-week dinners. I love these fritters served with a big bowl of salad tossed with our creamy tahini dressing (see page 98) or roast vegetables drizzled with salsa verde, chermoula or almond and tomato pesto (see pages 102, 110 and 112).

Makes 15

75g gram flour

1½ tsp baking powder

1 tsp ground cumin

300g carrots, peeled and coarsely grated

2 spring onions, peeled and finely sliced

10g coriander, finely chopped

1 tbsp sunflower or coconut oil

1. Sift the flour, baking powder and cumin into a large mixing bowl. Add the carrots, spring onions and coriander and season to taste. Stir everything together until you have a thick, fairly dry mixture. Set aside for 10 minutes.

2. Heat a little of the oil in a large, non-stick frying pan. Add tablespoons of the mixture and flatten into 1cm-thick patties, spacing them a little apart.

3. Cook for 3–4 minutes each side, until crisp and golden. Keep warm and repeat with the remaining mixture.

Note

Don't be alarmed by how thick the mixture is when you're making these – the moisture from the carrots will keep the fritters tender in the middle.

courgette and herb fritters

These are a go-to recipe on busy days. The mint, parsley, spring onions and garlic give the courgettes lots of flavour, and the gram (chickpea) flour adds great plant protein too.

Makes 16

400g courgettes, trimmed and coarsely grated

70g gram flour

1½ tsp baking powder

1 tbsp nutritional yeast

2 spring onions, finely sliced

1 garlic clove, crushed

small handful of flat-leaf parsley, finely chopped

2 mint sprigs, leaves finely chopped

1 tbsp sunflower or coconut oil

sea salt

To serve

salsa verde, chermoula or pesto (see pages 102, 110 and 112)

1. Sprinkle a little salt over the courgettes, place in a colander and set aside to drain for 15 minutes.

2. Sift the flour and baking powder into a large mixing bowl. Add the nutritional yeast, spring onion, garlic, parsley, and mint.

3. Squeeze as much liquid as possible out of the courgettes and add them to the bowl. Season to taste and stir the mixture to combine, ensuring that no dry patches of flour remain.

4. Heat a little of the oil in a large, non-stick frying pan. Add tablespoons of the mixture and flatten into 1cm-thick patties, spacing them a little apart. Cook for 4–5 minutes on each side, until crisp and golden. Keep warm under a tea towel and repeat with the remaining mixture.

Note

Courgettes hold a lot of water so it's important to really squeeze out as much liquid as you can before adding them to the fritter mixture. Letting them sit with the salt at the start really helps get that extra liquid out too, so don't skip that step!

Rohini's moong dhal

Serves 4

200g dried moong dal (split yellow lentils)

1 tsp extra virgin olive oil or rapeseed oil

1 tsp black mustard seeds

1 tsp ground turmeric

¼ tsp asafoetida powder (optional)

4–5 curry leaves, fresh or dried

3 garlic cloves, crushed

4cm piece of ginger, grated

1 large onion, finely chopped

3 green chillies, halved (remove the seeds if you don't like heat)

3 medium tomatoes, chopped

100g spinach leaves (optional)

40g coriander leaves

juice of 1 lemon

sea salt and black pepper

cucumber and mint raita (see page 109), to serve

1. Place the moong dal into a bowl, cover with water and leave to soak for an hour or two. Rinse thoroughly until the water runs clear, then drain. (You can skip the soaking step but the lentils may take slightly longer to cook.)

2. Bring 1.5 litres of water to the boil in a large saucepan and add the rinsed lentils, then turn down the heat to a simmer. Cook the lentils for 20–30 minutes or until they are very soft, stirring every 10 minutes or so.

3. Meanwhile, heat the oil in a deep saucepan until it's hot but not smoking. Reduce the heat and add the mustard seeds, turmeric and asafoetida (if using). Let them crackle for around 15 seconds.

4. Add the curry leaves, garlic and ginger with 2 tablespoons of hot water. Sauté for a minute then add the onion and chillies and sauté for a couple of minutes on a medium heat.

5. Add the tomatoes, stir and cover for 5 minutes.

6. Add the cooked lentils to the pan and bring the mixture to a boil, stirring everything thoroughly. Once boiling, turn down to a simmer. You can add a bit more liquid (1–2 ladlefuls of boiling water) if you aren't planning on serving the dhal straightaway as it tends to thicken up a bit as it cools. Cook for 5 minutes.

7. Remove the pan from the heat. Season to taste with salt and black pepper. Add the spinach (if using), coriander and lemon juice once the dhal has cooled slightly.

8. Serve the dhal on its own as a soup, or with brown basmati rice, quinoa or wholemeal chapatis. It pairs beautifully with the cucumber and mint raita (see page 109).

Shireen's chana bateta

Serves 4

500g potatoes, peeled and cut into bite-sized pieces

1 tsp olive or coconut oil

1 tsp black mustard seeds

4 curry leaves, fresh or dried

2 red chillies, finely chopped, seeds removed if desired

1 × 400g tin of chopped tomatoes

1 tbsp tomato purée

¼ teaspoon fine sea salt, or to taste

½ tsp ground turmeric

dried chilli flakes, to taste

2 tbsp gram flour

2 tbsp cold water

1 tbsp tamarind paste

2 × 400g tins of chickpeas, drained

juice of 1 lemon

1 tsp coconut sugar (optional)

cucumber and mint raita (see page 109), to serve

1. Place the potatoes in a large saucepan and cover with cold water. Place over a medium heat, bring to a gentle simmer and cook until you can pierce them with a fork and feel no resistance, but not so much that they begin to lose their shape. Drain well, spread out on a large plate to stop the cooking process and leave to cool while you make the sauce.

2. Place a large, heavy-bottomed pan over a medium–high heat and add the oil. Add the mustard seeds, curry leaves and red chilli and heat until the mustard seeds start popping. Add the tomatoes, tomato purée, salt, turmeric and chilli flakes to taste. Cook until darkened and reduced, stirring frequently (around 10–15 minutes).

3. To thicken the sauce, place the gram flour in a small bowl with the cold water, whisk until dissolved then add it to the sauce. Stir until well mixed.

4. Add the tamarind paste and mix again. Add the boiled potatoes and chickpeas and cook for a few minutes. Add hot water to loosen the sauce if needed. Add the lemon juice and remove the pan from the heat. If the sauce is too tart then add the sugar.

5. Serve the chana bateta while piping hot with cucumber and mint raita.

zingy 30-minute curry

This is deliciously zingy, with lots of lime and a saucy coconut mix made with our golden paste. Make the full amount of paste, use half in this recipe, then later in the week use the other half for the golden noodle bowls or spicy sweet potato soup (see pages 161 and 163).

Serves 4

1 × 300g block of firm tofu

1 tbsp toasted sesame oil

1 red onion, diced

5 tbsp golden paste (about half the batch; see page 122)

200g baby corn, chopped into bite-sized pieces

1 × 400ml tin of coconut milk

2 tsp coconut sugar

150g mangetout, trimmed

75g frozen edamame beans

2 juicy limes, 3 if they're less juicy

sea salt

To serve

jasmine rice

coriander

1 lime, cut into wedges

dollop of coconut yoghurt (optional)

1. Drain and dry the block of tofu. The easiest way to do it is to wrap the tofu in a tea towel, then place it on a chopping board with something heavy on top, such as a book or heavy frying pan. Leave it for about 10 minutes – this will press out the excess water – then cut into bite sized pieces.

2. While the tofu drains, place a large frying pan over a medium heat and add the sesame oil. Once it's warm, add the red onion with a sprinkling of sea salt. Cook for 5–10 minutes, until softened.

3. Next add the golden paste and cook for 2–3 minutes, to cook off the spices and shallot, then add the corn, tofu, coconut milk and coconut sugar. Bring to the boil, then turn the heat down to a simmer. Add the mangetout. Leave to simmer for 15 minutes, until the corn is cooked. Add the edamame and cook for 3 minutes or so, until the edamame is cooked.

4. Add the lime juice, season to taste and serve with jasmine rice, lots of coriander, lime wedges and a dollop of coconut yoghurt, if wished.

warming golden noodles

This was one of the first recipes I made for this book and it really gave me confidence in the project, as I just kept coming back to it time and time again. It only takes 10 minutes to prep, and then you just let it simmer away as you potter around the house. The paste makes two meals' worth, so either make this again later in the week, switching up the veg, or try the golden sweet potato soup or zingy 30-minute curry (see pages 158 and 163).

Serves 4

1 tbsp sesame oil

1 shallot (you can use onions, but shallots give it a sweeter, more subtle flavour)

4 garlic cloves, finely chopped

5 tbsp golden paste (see page 122)

200ml boiling water

2 × 400ml tins of coconut milk

1 tsp coconut sugar

180g soba noodles

100g frozen edamame beans

150g mangetout or sugar snap peas

2 big handfuls of bean sprouts

sea salt

fresh coriander, to serve

1–2 limes, to serve

1. Pour the sesame oil into a saucepan over a medium heat, add the shallots, fry for 2 minutes or so, then add the garlic and a sprinkling of salt. Cook for a further 5 minutes, until soft. Add the paste and cook for another 2 minutes, making sure to cook off the spices and shallot.

2. Add the boiling water – this will clean the bottom of the pan and absorb all those flavours – then add the coconut milk and coconut sugar.

3. Bring to the boil, cover and simmer on a low heat for 45 minutes to 1 hour – the longer it cooks the deeper the flavour will be.

4. About 10 minutes before serving, cook the noodles according to the instructions on the pack. Add the veg for the last 2 minutes. Drain the noodles and veg and divide them between four bowls. Pour in the broth and top with a sprinkling of fresh coriander, a big squeeze of lime and some salt to taste.

golden sweet potato and lentil soup

An easy midweek dinner that's beautifully warming and comforting. With lime juice, miso, our spicy golden paste and red lentils, all blended with a little coconut yoghurt to make it extra creamy. I serve it with an extra dollop of thick coconut yoghurt and a big handful of crunchy croutons (see page 98).

1 tsp coconut oil

1 red onion, diced

5 tbsp golden paste (about half the batch; see page 122)

2 large sweet potatoes (about 500g), peeled and cut into bite-sized chunks

75g red lentils, rinsed

1 tsp coconut sugar

500ml boiling water

1 tsp brown rice miso

2 tbsp coconut yoghurt

2 tbsp tomato purée

200ml unsweetened almond milk

juice of 1 juicy lime

sea salt and black pepper

To serve

crunchy croutons (see page 98)

coconut yoghurt

1. Place a large saucepan on a medium heat and add the coconut oil. Once the oil has melted, add the red onion with a sprinkling of salt. Let the onion cook for about 5 minutes, until it starts to soften, then add the golden paste and cook for a further 3 minutes or so, to cook off the spices and shallot.

2. Add the sweet potatoes, red lentils and coconut sugar stirring them through the paste for a minute or two.

3. Add the boiling water. Turn the heat up, bringing the pan to the boil, cover and turn the heat down. Let the soup simmer for 20 minutes, until the sweet potatoes are tender.

4. Add the miso, yoghurt, tomato purée, almond milk and lime juice. Remove the pan from the heat and blend the soup using a stick blender until smooth and creamy. Season to taste. Serve with crispy croutons and coconut yoghurt.

Alan's creamy green sauerkraut soup

With a true diversity of plants and the microbiome-boosting powers of fermented sauerkraut, this comforting soup is a treat for you and your gut microbes. Traditional sauerkraut soup recipes call for the kraut to be added along with the other veggies, so that it cooks and softens, but I prefer to add it last to preserve the bacteria. Serve with a good wholegrain bread topped with hummus.

Serves 4

1 onion, roughly chopped

1 tsp extra virgin olive oil (optional)

2 garlic cloves, finely chopped

160g broccoli, cut into florets

160g cauliflower, cut into florets

1 litre vegetable stock

2 handfuls of baby leaf spinach

1 tbsp nutritional yeast

1 tbsp dried mixed herbs

1 tsp Dijon mustard

250–300g sauerkraut (drain and rinse, or leave as it is to add tang to the soup)

250g plain soya yoghurt

black pepper

1. Put the onion into a saucepan over a medium–low heat with the olive oil or a dash of water. Cook it for 3 minutes, then add the garlic and cook it for another minute (add a dash of water if it is catching).

2. Add the broccoli, cauliflower and stock. Bring to the boil and simmer for 15–20 minutes.

3. Add the spinach, nutritional yeast, mixed herbs and Dijon mustard. Turn the heat down to low and stir the soup for a minute.

4. Remove the pan from the heat and roughly blend the soup a bit using a stick-blender, leaving some of the veg florets whole.

5. Stir in the yoghurt, until well combined.

6. Pour the soup into bowls and top with the sauerkraut, gently stirring some of it through each bowl. Top with black pepper and serve immediately.

everyday minestrone

A chunky, hearty soup that's become a staple in our house. May, our youngest daughter, absolutely loves this recipe. It's delicious as it is, but feel free to mix and match the veg, depending on what you've got in the house. You can replace the courgette with green beans and swap the tinned tomatoes for fresh in the summer.

Serves 4

1 tbsp olive oil

1 onion, finely chopped (or a large leek, washed and finely chopped)

2 carrots, peeled and finely chopped

2 celery sticks, finely chopped

small bunch of basil, stalks finely chopped, leaves reserved

2 garlic cloves, finely sliced

2 tbsp tomato purée

1 large courgette, roughly chopped

1 × 400g tin of cannellini beans, drained and rinsed

1 × 400g tin of chopped tomatoes

1 fresh bay leaf

1 litre hot vegetable stock

100g short pasta, such as macaroni

sea salt and black pepper

1. Heat the olive oil in a large saucepan or casserole over a high heat, then add the onion, carrots, celery and basil stalks and season well with salt and pepper.

2. Turn the heat down a little, cover the pan with a lid and sweat the vegetables for 10 minutes until they are soft.

3. Add the sliced garlic and cook for another couple of minutes.

4. Stir in the tomato purée, courgette, cannellini beans, chopped tomatoes, bay leaf and 500ml of the vegetable stock. Season again, turn up the heat, bring to the boil and simmer for 10 minutes.

5. Add the pasta and remaining vegetable stock and simmer until the pasta is cooked – around 8 minutes.

6. Finely chop the basil leaves and stir through. Add a little more water if the soup is too thick.

Note
This is great topped with the crunchy croutons on page 98.

from the oven

simple summer tray bake

This is a perfect meal on a warm day. It couldn't be simpler to make, there's almost no prep and barely any washing up, but it's still packed with flavour. I serve it with a simple salad tossed with the creamy tahini dressing on page 98 or one of the pestos on page 112 – it's particularly good with the rocket and pistachio pesto.

Serves 4

1 large red onion or 2 small, peeled and sliced into slim wedges

2 garlic cloves, bashed with the flat of your knife

400g cherry tomatoes

2 red peppers, deseeded and finely sliced

1 × 400g tin of chickpeas, drained and rinsed

1 aubergine, cut into 2cm chunks

2 rosemary sprigs

3 tbsp olive oil

1½ tbsp balsamic vinegar

150g sourdough, torn into bite-sized chunks

sea salt and black pepper

To serve

handful of basil, leaves roughly torn

drizzle of pesto (of your choice; see page 112)

green salad tossed with creamy tahini dressing (page 98)

1. Preheat the oven to 200°C fan.

2. Put the onion, garlic, cherry tomatoes, peppers, chickpeas, aubergine and rosemary into a large roasting tin (approximately 30 × 25cm). Pour over 2 tbsp of the oil, season to your taste and roast for 20 minutes.

3. Add the remaining oil and the balsamic vinegar to a mixing bowl and tip in the chunks of bread. Toss the bread in the oil and vinegar mixture until well coated.

4. Once the vegetables have roasted for 20 minutes, gently turn them, then scatter the bread over the top. Return to the oven and bake for a further 10 minutes, until the vegetables are tender and golden, and the bread is crisp. Discard the rosemary and slip the garlic cloves out of their sins, once they are cool enough to handle.

5. Serve scattered with fresh basil, a drizzle of pesto and a simple green salad tossed in tahini dressing.

peanutty aubergine tray bake

This dish combines the deliciously ella community's three favourite ingredients – peanut butter, aubergines and sweet potatoes – to make a real crowd-pleaser. Served with lots of fresh herbs, chilli and spring onion, it's vibrant and absolutely delicious.

Serves 4

2 large aubergines, cut lengthways into wedges (about 30 wedges)

2 large sweet potatoes, cut into wedges the same size as the aubergine

½ tsp cinnamon

½ tsp sweet smoked paprika

¼ tsp cayenne pepper

1 tbsp olive oil

1 tsp maple syrup

sea salt

For the dressing

juice of 1 lime

1 tbsp maple syrup

1 tbsp toasted sesame oil

3 tbsp smooth, creamy peanut butter (see Note, below)

1 tsp tamari or soy sauce

½ garlic clove, crushed

To serve

handful of mint, finely chopped

handful of coriander, finely chopped

handful of dill, finely chopped

1 red chilli, finely sliced

3 spring onions, finely sliced

2 tbsp roasted peanuts

2 tbsp sesame seeds

a crisp green salad and/or steamed jasmine rice

1. Preheat the oven to 180°C fan.

2. Place the aubergine and sweet potato wedges in a bowl and toss with the spices, olive oil, maple syrup and some salt, ensuring everything is evenly coated.

3. Add the sweet potatoes to a large baking tray, place in the oven and roast for 10 minutes.

4. Add the aubergines to the tray, ensuring they're evenly spread across it as they'll go soggy if they're piled on top of each other. Roast for 35–40 minutes, until the veg is tender and starting to turn a little golden brown.

5. While the vegetables are cooking, make the dressing by whisking all of the ingredients together until smooth.

6. To finish, drizzle the dressing over the veg. Top with the herbs, chilli, spring onions, peanuts and sesame seeds. Serve with a green salad and/or steamed jasmine rice.

Note

If your peanut butter is quite firm you can loosen it with a little hot water before adding it to the dressing.

cauliflower and cashew pilaf tray bake

The ginger, garlic, bay leaves and spices give this cauliflower and cashew pilaf loads of depth, with a nice pop of colour from the green beans. I love it with a little drizzle of harissa, for a gentle hint of spice.

Serves 4

1 onion, finely sliced

1 cauliflower, tough outer leaves discarded, cut into florets

1 thumb-sized piece of ginger, peeled and finely grated

2 garlic cloves, crushed

1½ tbsp coconut oil, melted

1 cinnamon stick

2 bay leaves

1 tsp cumin seeds

½ tsp turmeric

1 tsp ground coriander

50g cashews, roughly chopped

40g sultanas

250g white basmati rice, rinsed and drained

200g green beans, trimmed and cut into 4–5cm lengths

500ml hot vegetable stock

1 lemon, halved

small handful of coriander, roughly chopped

harissa (page 104), to serve (optional)

1. Preheat the oven to 180°C fan.

2. Put the onion, cauliflower, ginger and garlic into a large roasting tin. Add the coconut oil, cinnamon, bay leaves, cumin, turmeric, coriander and cashews. Mix everything until well combined and spread out in a single, even layer.

3. Place the tray in the oven and bake for 10 minutes, until the onion and cauliflower have taken on a little colour.

4. Take the tray out and add the sultanas, rice and green beans. Stir them through the veg, then spread everything out in an even layer. Pour over the hot stock.

5. Cover the tray with foil and bake for 25–30 minutes, until the cauliflower and rice are tender. Season and add a squeeze of lemon juice to taste, then serve with a generous sprinkling of coriander, and a drizzle of harissa, if you like.

Note

To vary this, you can swap the cauliflower for squash or sweet potato – just peel and chop into bite-sized pieces and add it in the same way.

Tip for tinies

If you're cooking for very young children, omit the cashews from the roasting tin and sprinkle over the adults' portions when serving.

piri piri tray bake

This simple dinner is absolutely packed with flavour. The roasted paprika and garlic potato wedges, corn and red peppers are delicious served with a green salad and a generous drizzling of either chermoula or harissa (see pages 110 and 104).

Serves 4

3 large baking potatoes, scrubbed and cut into wedges

4 tbsp olive oil

1 large red onion, peeled and sliced into slim wedges

2 red peppers, deseeded and sliced

4 garlic cloves, roughly chopped

1 red chilli (or to taste), deseeded and roughly chopped

1 tbsp sweet smoked paprika

small handful of fresh oregano leaves (stems discarded)

1 tbsp red wine or apple cider vinegar

4 whole corn cobs, halved widthways

1 lemon, cut into wedges

To serve

green salad

chermoula, harissa or almond and tomato pesto (see pages 110 and 104 and 112)

1. Preheat the oven to 180°C fan.

2. Pat the potatoes dry with kitchen paper and transfer to a large roasting tin (approximately 30 × 25cm). Pour over half of the olive oil and season to your taste. Spread the potatoes out into a single, even layer and bake for 20 minutes, while you prepare the piri piri sauce.

3. Blend half the onion with one of the peppers, the garlic, chilli, paprika, oregano leaves, vinegar and remaining olive oil. Once smooth, season to taste.

4. Tip the remaining pepper and the corn into a mixing bowl and pour over the piri piri sauce.

5. Once the potatoes have cooked for 20 minutes, remove the tray from the oven. Turn the potatoes, so that they cook evenly, and add the piri piri coated veg to the tin. Bake for a further 20–25 minutes, until the vegetables are just tender and golden.

6. Remove from the oven and serve with a simple green salad and a drizzle of chermoula, harissa or pesto for extra flavour.

Tip for tinies

Leave out the red chilli and serve with a little of the almond and tomato pesto instead of harissa or chermoula.

roasted squash and tomato dhal tray bake

A family friendly one-pan wonder that's on regular rotation in our house. It's gentle and soothing – everything you need after a long day. I serve it with coconut yoghurt, fresh coriander and chilli flakes.

Serves 4

1 red onion, finely sliced

1 butternut squash, deseeded, peeled and cut into 3cm chunks

1 thumb-sized piece of ginger, peeled and finely grated

2 garlic cloves, crushed

¼ tsp ground turmeric

1 tbsp mild curry powder

1½ tbsp olive oil

200g red lentils, washed and drained

1 × 400g tin of chopped tomatoes

1 × 400g tin of coconut milk

250ml hot vegetable stock

1 lemon, halved

sea salt and black pepper

To serve

coconut yoghurt

small handful of coriander, roughly chopped

pinch of dried chilli flakes (optional)

1. Preheat the oven to 180°C fan.

2. Put the onion, squash, ginger, garlic, turmeric and curry powder into a large roasting tray. Drizzle over the olive oil and season with a teaspoon of sea salt and a generous amount of black pepper. Toss everything together so that it's all nicely coated, then spread out in a single, even layer.

3. Place the tray in the oven and bake for 10–12 minutes, until the squash and onion have taken on a little colour.

4. Remove the tray from the oven and add the lentils, tomatoes, coconut milk and stock. Stir well and return to the oven for 30 minutes, until the squash is just tender and the lentils are soft.

5. Season and squeeze over some lemon juice to taste, then serve with a dollop of coconut yoghurt, a sprinkling of coriander and chili flakes (if using).

miso aubergine and squash tray bake

Baked with ginger, coriander, miso, spring onion and garlic, these aubergines are bursting with flavour. The smooth, creamy garlicky yoghurt, tender roasted squash and baby spinach balance their richness though, creating a delicious dinner.

Serves 4

2 aubergines, halved lengthways

1 large red onion, peeled and cut into wedges

1 butternut squash (about 800g), skin on, deseeded and cut into ½ cm slices

3 tbsp olive oil

2 garlic cloves, roughly chopped

2 tbsp brown rice miso

25g coriander leaves and stalks, roughly chopped

2cm piece of ginger, peeled and roughly chopped

4 spring onions, roughly chopped

1 × 400g tin of green lentils, drained

200g baby leaf spinach

sea salt and black pepper

sliced lime, to serve

For the garlicky coconut yoghurt

150g coconut yoghurt

1 garlic clove, crushed

1 tbsp extra virgin olive oil

1 tbsp tahini

1. Preheat the oven to 180°C fan.

2. Score the aubergine flesh in a criss-cross pattern, sprinkle some salt over the flesh and set aside for 15 minutes.

3. Mix the onion wedges, squash slices and 2 tablespoons of the olive oil in a large bowl. Season with salt and pepper and spread out in a large, deep roasting tray. Roast in the oven for 15 minutes.

4. Place the garlic, miso, coriander, ginger, spring onions, the remaining tablespoon of olive oil and 1 tablespoon of water to a food processor and blitz for a couple of minutes until you have a paste.

5. Rinse and pat the aubergines dry then spread the paste over the cut side of the flesh. Put the aubergines on top of the squash and onions and return to the oven for 30 minutes.

6. Scatter the lentils around the roasted vegetables, tuck the spinach under the aubergines and return to the oven for another 5 minutes.

7. To make the yoghurt, mix all the ingredients together and season with salt.

8. Serve the aubergine and vegetables with a spoonful of garlicky yoghurt and some slices of lime.

one-tray nachos

Everything you need for movie nights or a lazy Saturday meal.
These are a real crowd-pleaser, full of everyone's favourites – tortilla chips,
avocado, cashew cream and black beans.

Serves 4

1 large red onion or 2 small, peeled and sliced into slim wedges

2 garlic cloves, crushed

400g cherry tomatoes

1 × 400g tin of black beans, drained and rinsed

1 tsp ground cumin

1½ tsp sweet smoked paprika

1½ tbsp olive oil

1 × 170g pack lightly salted tortilla chips

smooth cashew cream (see page 107)

2 ripe avocados, peeled, halved, stoned and sliced into bite-sized pieces

handful of coriander, roughly chopped

1 red chili, finely sliced

sea salt and black pepper

1 lime, to serve

1. Preheat the oven to 180°C fan.

2. Add the onion, garlic, tomatoes, beans, cumin and smoked paprika to a roasting tin, approximately 30 × 25cm. Drizzle with olive oil, season lightly (the tortillas will be fairly salty) and toss to coat everything in the spices and oil.

3. Spread everything out in a single, even layer. Place the tray in the oven and bake for 30–35 minutes, until the tomatoes have begun to break down.

4. Either serve in the tin, or transfer it to a flat-ish serving dish. Scatter the tortilla chips around the edge of the tin and top with the cashew cream (see Tip, below, to make it even more delicious), avocado, coriander and chili slices, followed by a squeeze of lime and sprinkling of salt.

Tip

Try adding ¼ teaspoon of sweet smoked paprika to the smooth cashew cream; it tastes amazing.

easy root veg tray bake

This sounds simple but it's truly delicious, and always leaves me feeling both satisfied and nourished. It's most delicious (and looks best) with baby vegetables, but that's not a must by any means – simply swap them for regular-sized veg and cut them into quarters lengthways. It's important to keep the chunks of swede fairly small, so that they cook in the same time as the other veg.

Serves 4

300g baby parsnips, scrubbed and halved lengthways

200g baby carrots, scrubbed and halved lengthways

250g swede or squash, cut into 2cm chunks

275g new potatoes, scrubbed and halved

1 red onion, peeled and sliced into slim wedges

2 garlic cloves, peeled

½ tsp ground cinnamon

1 tsp ground cumin

3 tbsp olive oil

100g kale, leaves stripped from stalks and roughly shredded

1 tbsp nutritional yeast

seeds from ½ pomegranate (about 75g)

sea salt and black pepper

herby dressing (see page 94) or salsa verde (see page 102), to serve

1. Preheat the oven to 180°C fan.

2. Tip the parsnips, carrots, swede, new potatoes, onion, garlic, cinnamon and cumin into a large roasting tin (about 30 × 25cm). Pour over 2 tablespoons of the olive oil, season to your taste and roast for 30 minutes.

3. Turn the oven down to 160°C fan.

4. Toss the kale with the remaining oil and nutritional yeast. Scatter the kale over the vegetables and bake for a further 10 minutes, until the vegetables are just tender and the kale is crisp at the edges (keep an eye on the kale as it can burn easily).

5. Sprinkle over the pomegranate seeds and serve with the herby dressing or salsa verde.

orzo veggie tray bake

This is a delicious, veggie-packed dinner that couldn't be easier to make. Cooking the orzo with veggie stock, garlic, spring onions, roast tomatoes and courgette means it's bursting with flavour. We make this a lot at home, it's a huge hit with our little ones. It's delicious with our rocket and pistachio pesto (page 112).

Serves 4

500g courgettes, cut into 1.5cm thick slices, on the diagonal

250g cherry tomatoes

1½ tbsp olive oil

4 spring onions, trimmed and finely sliced

2 garlic cloves, peeled and crushed

300g orzo

600ml vegetable stock

1 tbsp nutritional yeast

handful of flat-leaf parsley, roughly chopped

sea salt and black pepper

To serve

rocket and pistachio pesto (see page 112)

fresh basil

1. Preheat the oven to 200°C fan.

2. Tip the courgettes and cherry tomatoes into a large roasting tin (about 30 × 25cm). Pour over the olive oil, season to taste and toss until everything has a light coating of oil. Roast for 10 minutes.

3. Add the spring onion and garlic to the tin and roast for a further 2 minutes, until fragrant. Add the orzo, vegetable stock, nutritional yeast and parsley and stir gently, so that the vegetables sit on top of the orzo. Return to the oven and bake for 20 minutes, until the orzo is tender and the liquid has been absorbed.

4. Serve with a drizzle of the pesto and some fresh basil.

gnocchi and butter bean bake

I make this a lot when I'm short on time during the week but still need something really delicious, filling and relatively simple that I can share with friends or family. The cashew cream makes the dish, adding a deliciously creamy contrast to the rich tomato sauce.

Serves 4–6

1 red onion, finely sliced

3 garlic cloves, finely chopped

400g cherry tomatoes

1 tbsp olive oil

1 tsp dried basil

1 × 450g pack of gnocchi

1 × 400g tin of butter beans, drained

400g passata (or you can blend a tin of chopped tomatoes until smooth)

100g smooth cashew cream (see page 107)

50ml oat milk

2 tbsp nutritional yeast

few leaves of fresh basil

sea salt and black pepper

1. Preheat the oven to 180°C fan.

2. Place the red onion, garlic and cherry tomatoes in a 25 × 30 cm baking dish. Add the olive oil, dried basil, some salt and pepper and toss to combine. Bake in the oven for about 20 minutes, until softened and tender.

3. Remove the dish from the oven and add the gnocchi, butter beans and passata. Stir to combine and place back in the oven for a further 25 minutes.

4. Meanwhile, whisk together the cashew cream, oat milk and nutritional yeast until combined. Remove from the oven and drizzle over the creamy cashew sauce, then return and bake for a further 5 minutes until darkened, reduced and bubbling at the edges.

5. Remove from the oven and allow to cool for 5 minutes before serving. Top with fresh basil leaves and flaky sea salt to taste.

crispy buffalo cauliflower tray bake

The herby dressing brings this dish together. It's brilliantly vibrant and creamy, and goes perfectly with the crisp butter lettuce, crunchy roasted chickpeas, chunks of avocado, slices of red onion, cherry tomatoes and the crispy cauliflower florets.

Serves 4

200g plain flour

350ml oat milk

1 large cauliflower (about 750g), cut into medium-sized florets

sea salt and black pepper

For the coating

200g plain flour

2 tsp paprika

2 tsp garlic powder

1 tsp ground cumin

1 tsp cayenne pepper

½ tsp cinnamon

For the chickpeas

1 × 400g tin of chickpeas, drained

2 tbsp olive oil, plus extra for drizzling

2 tsp ground cumin

1 tsp chilli flakes

To serve

1 head of butter lettuce

200g cherry tomatoes, quartered

1 red onion, thinly sliced

2 ripe avocados, cut into bite-sized chunks

herby dressing (see page 94)

1. Preheat the oven to 200°C fan.

2. Mix the flour and oat milk in a large mixing bowl with some salt, until smooth. Then mix the coating ingredients in a separate bowl.

3. Dip the cauliflower florets into the flour and oat mixture, shake off any excess, then roll in the coating, ensuring each floret is fully covered.

4. Place the florets on a large, lined baking sheet and roast for 35 minutes, turning halfway through the cooking time. Make sure each floret has space; if they sit on top of each other they won't be crunchy.

5. Meanwhile, toss the chickpeas with olive oil, cumin and chilli flakes. Add them to the cauliflower tray when you take it out to turn the florets halfway through their cooking time.

6. Five minutes before the end of the cooking time, remove the tray from the oven and drizzle the cauliflower with olive oil, before returning it for a final 5 minutes to crisp up. Don't worry if some of the oil goes on to the chickpeas.

7. Once the cauliflower is nice and crispy, remove the tray from the oven and let it cool for a few minutes. To serve, pile the lettuce, tomatoes, onion and avocado into the tray, and drizzle everything (generously) with the herby dressing. Season to taste.

simple baked ratatouille

This looks simple, but it's so delicious and is always such a hit. Having everything in one pan makes life a lot easier too. If you have any leftovers, blitz them in a food processor and toss through spaghetti the next day – they make a wonderful sauce.

Serves 4

1 large aubergine, sliced into 0.5cm rounds

1 tbsp olive oil, plus extra for drizzling

1 red onion, thinly sliced

2 garlic cloves, thinly sliced

1 tsp dried thyme

500ml passata + 50ml water to rinse out the container

1 tbsp balsamic vinegar

1 yellow pepper, deseeded and sliced into 0.5cm rounds

2 medium courgettes, sliced into 0.5cm rounds

sea salt and black pepper

1. Preheat the oven to 180°C fan.

2. Arrange the aubergine slices in a colander (place it over a bowl to keep the counter dry) and sprinkle with one teaspoon of salt. Leave it to one side while you prep the sauce.

3. Place a casserole dish (about 25–30cm in diameter and preferably a shallow one) over a medium heat and gently heat the olive oil. Add the onion and fry for 5–10 minutes until soft, season with salt and pepper then add the garlic and fry for another couple of minutes.

4. Add the thyme, passata, water and balsamic vinegar; turn up the heat and bring to the boil. Let it bubble for 2–3 minutes then remove from the heat.

5. Rinse and pat the aubergine dry using kitchen paper.

6. Arrange the aubergine, yellow pepper and courgette in a spiral on top of the tomato sauce, overlapping them slightly and alternating the vegetables until they are all used up. Drizzle a little more olive oil over the top, season with salt and pepper, then bake in the oven, uncovered, for 30 minutes, until the vegetables are slightly charred and the sauce is thick. Serve immediately.

Tip for tinies
For very little ones, blitz their portion to make a veggie sauce.

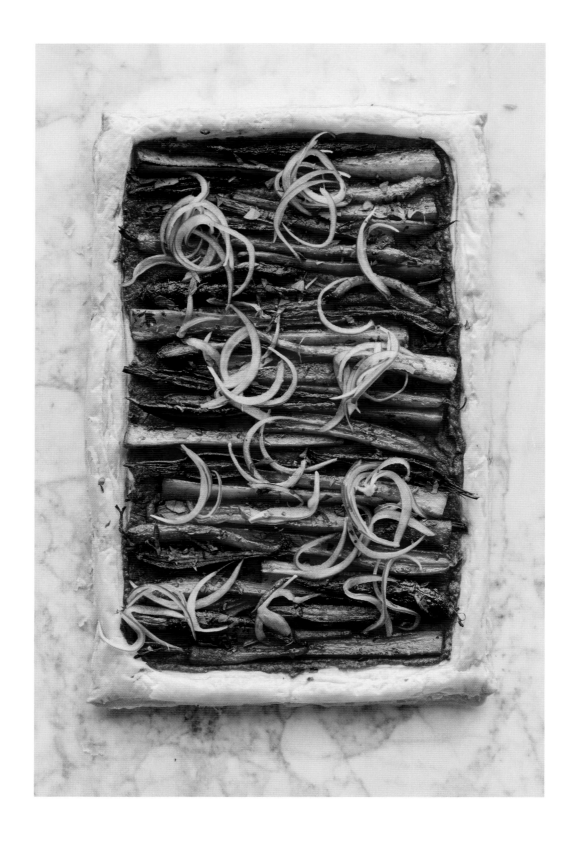

root veg and pickled red onion tart

This is a beautiful tart and I tend to use it as a simple showstopper. It's delicious served with a spinach salad tossed in our creamy tahini dressing (see page 98).

Serves 4

300g baby carrots, peeled and halved lengthways

300g parsnips, peeled and cut into 10 × 1cm batons

1 tbsp brown rice miso

2 tbsp maple syrup

1 tbsp olive oil

1 × 320g sheet of ready-rolled vegan puff pastry

150g roasted walnut and red pepper dip (see page 115)

small bunch of parsley, finely chopped, to serve

For the pastry wash

1 tbsp oat milk

¼ tsp maple syrup

For the pickled red onion

2 tbsp red wine vinegar

1 tsp salt

½ tsp maple syrup

½ red onion, finely sliced

1. Preheat the oven to 180°C fan.

2. Mix together the carrots, parsnips, miso, maple syrup and olive oil.

3. Heat a deep, lidded frying pan over a medium heat and add the carrots and parsnips along with 4 tablespoons of water. Bring the liquid to the boil then cover, turn the heat down and steam for 5 minutes.

4. Spread the pastry out on a baking tray. Score the edges to give a 2cm border.

5. Spread the walnut and pepper dip over the pastry, leaving the border free. Mix the ingredients for the pastry wash and brush it over the borders.

6. Remove the carrots and parsnips from the frying pan with a slotted spoon and arrange on top of the pastry, reserving the liquid in the pan. Bake the tart for 30 minutes, until the crust starts to go golden.

7. While the tart bakes, mix the vinegar, salt and maple syrup in a small bowl. Add the onions and put to one side to pickle.

8. Remove the tart from the oven. Heat the reserved liquid from the carrots and parsnips in the frying pan and let it bubble for a minute or so until you have a thick sauce. Brush this all over the tart filling.

9. Sprinkle over the pickled red onions and chopped parsley and serve immediately.

creamy leek crumble

This dish is a sort of macaroni-and-cheese meets cauliflower cheese and potato dauphinois. It's rich, creamy, comforting and perfect for sharing with friends and family. The crisp crumble topping is a perfect contrast to the soft, creamy filling.

Serves 4 (or 8 as a side)

100g cashews

400ml hot vegetable stock

2 Maris Piper potatoes (450g), peeled and cut into 2cm cubes

1 small cauliflower (400g), cut into small florets, leaves retained and shredded

1 tbsp olive oil

2 onions, roughly chopped

2 large leeks (500g), finely sliced

2 garlic cloves, finely chopped or crushed

100ml oat milk

1 × 400g tin of cannellini beans, drained

5 tbsp nutritional yeast

1½ tbsp Dijon mustard

1 lemon, zest and juice

25g bunch of chives, finely chopped

75g porridge oats

2 slices sourdough (about 150g), blitzed into breadcrumbs

50ml coconut oil, melted

4 tbsp mixed seeds

flaky sea salt

1. Soak the cashews in the hot vegetable stock for an hour until softened.

2. Heat the oven to 220°C fan. Fill a large saucepan with cold water, add a generous pinch of salt and the potatoes, bring to the boil and turn down to a simmer. Simmer for 3 minutes and then add in the cauliflower florets, continuing to simmer for 4 minutes until the potatoes and cauliflower are starting to soften, then drain.

3. Meanwhile put the olive oil into a frying pan over a medium heat and add the onion, leeks and shredded cauliflower leaves and fry for 5–8 minutes until softened. Add the garlic and fry for another 30 seconds. Add the cannellini beans and mix until combined.

4. Tip a quarter of the cannellini mixture into a blender and add the soaked cashews and stock, oat milk, nutritional yeast, mustard and lemon, a quarter of the cauliflower and the potatoes, and some seasoning. Blitz on a high speed until you have a very smooth sauce.

5. Put the remaining cauliflower, potato and cannellini mixture into a large baking dish. Spoon over the creamy sauce and most of the chives (saving some to garnish) into a large baking dish, spreading it out to level.

6. Combine the oats, breadcrumbs, coconut oil, seeds, a generous pinch of salt and 60ml water in a bowl and mix with your hands, pressing everything together until you have a crumbly mixture. Scatter on top of the creamy filling and bake for 15–20 minutes until golden and heated through. Sprinkle over the remaining chives and a little flaky sea salt.

greens with salsa verde jacket potatoes

The beauty of this recipe is that the filling takes literally 5–10 minutes to prep. The greens are quickly blanched and tossed in olive oil and salt, then served with salsa verde in a fluffy jacket potato. A little sprinkling of dukkah adds extra flavour and a gentle crunch.

Serves 4

4 baking potatoes

olive oil, for coating the potatoes

salsa verde (see page 102)

250g purple sprouting broccoli, trimmed

500g spring greens, sliced into ribbons, or shredded kale

2 tbsp extra virgin olive oil

sea salt

dukkah (see page 101), to serve

1. Preheat the oven to 190°C fan. Rub the potatoes all over with a little olive oil and sea salt and bake on a baking tray for 60–90 mins, until crispy on the outside and soft in the middle.

2. Prepare the salsa verde following the method on page 102.

3. Bring a large pan of water to the boil and blanch the broccoli for 3–4 minutes then add the spring greens and cook for another minute. Strain the greens then return them to the empty pan and gently toss with the extra virgin olive oil and salt.

4. Serve piles of greens on top of each jacket potato with a good spoonful of salsa verde and a sprinkling of dukkah. Simple, quick and so delicious!

harissa chickpea jacket potatoes

Jacket potatoes are a brilliant midweek meals; they're filling, hearty, simple to make and so versatile. These harissa chickpeas take just 15 minutes to make, and are so delicious served with a sprinkling of dukkah or toasted seeds and a big dollop of garlicky coconut yoghurt.

Serves 4

4 baking potatoes

1 tbsp olive oil, plus extra for the potatoes

1 red onion, finely sliced

2 garlic cloves, crushed

small bunch of coriander, leaves and stalks separated and finely chopped

1 tsp ground cumin

2 × 400g tins of chickpeas, drained

4 tsp harissa (see page 104)

200g spinach, roughly chopped

juice of ½ lemon

sea salt and black pepper

To serve

garlicky coconut yoghurt (see page 181)

extra virgin olive oil

dukkah (see page 101)

1. Preheat the oven to 190°C fan. Rub the potatoes all over with a little olive oil and sea salt and bake on a baking tray for 60–90 mins, until crispy on the outside and soft in the middle.

2. Fifteen minutes before the potatoes are ready, make the chickpeas. Heat the olive oil in a large frying pan over a medium heat and add the onion. Fry for 5–7 minutes, until soft and beginning to caramelise.

3. Add the garlic and fry for another minute or so then stir in the coriander stalks and cumin. Fry again for another minute then mix in the chickpeas and harissa and season well with salt and pepper.

4. Add a splash of water to loosen and squash down some of the chickpeas with a wooden spoon. Add the spinach and cook until wilted.

5. Stir in the lemon juice and coriander leaves and serve immediately in crispy jacket potatoes topped with the garlicky yoghurt, extra virgin olive oil and a sprinkling of dukkah.

crispy corn and lentil jacket potatoes

The crispy corn really makes this recipe, creating the perfect contrast between the sour cream, soft chunks of avocado, juicy bites of fresh tomato, spicy chilli, and the fluffy baked potato. Perfect for warm spring evenings and summer barbecues.

Serves 4

4 baking potatoes

olive oil, for coating the potatoes

For the lentil salad

1 × 400g tin of green lentils

250g cherry tomatoes, quartered

1 avocado, roughly chopped

1 hot red chilli, deseeded and finely chopped

25g herb of your choice (parsley, coriander, mint or dill)

2 tbsp extra virgin olive oil

juice of 1 lime

sea salt and black pepper

For the speedy sour cream

200g coconut yoghurt

juice of ½ lemon

1 garlic clove, crushed

½ tsp salt

For the crispy corn

1 × 325g tin of sweetcorn, drained

3 tbsp cornflour

300ml sunflower oil

1. Preheat the oven to 190°C fan. Rub the potatoes all over with a little olive oil and sea salt and bake on a baking tray for 60–90 mins, until crispy on the outside and soft in the middle.

2. Mix the lentil salad ingredients together in a large bowl and set aside.

3. Mix the sour cream ingredients together in a small bowl and set aside.

4. Suspend a sieve over a bowl then toss the drained sweetcorn in the cornflour and tip into the sieve. This will keep the sweetcorn from getting too wet which can cause hot oil to spit aggressively.

5. Heat the sunflower oil to 180°C in a deep saucepan. Using a slotted spoon, fry the sweetcorn in batches for 3-4 minutes until crispy and golden. Transfer to a baking tray lined with a clean cloth or kitchen paper while you fry the rest of the corn. Serve the lentil salad over thejacket potatoes, topped with a spoonful of sour cream and the crispy corn.

black bean
jacket potatoes

Made with simple, store-cupboard ingredients, this recipe makes a hearty, comforting dinner. Simmering the black beans in veggie stock with cherry tomatoes, garlic, coriander, chilli and red onion gives each mouthful loads of flavour.

Serves 4

4 baking potatoes

1 tbsp olive oil, plus extra for the potatoes

1 red onion, finely chopped

2 garlic cloves, finely chopped

200g cherry tomatoes, halved

2 tsp ground coriander

pinch of dried chilli flakes

2 × 400g tins black beans, drained

200ml hot vegetable stock

small bunch of coriander (about 10g), leaves and stalks finely chopped

sea salt

lime wedges, to serve

1. Preheat the oven to 190°C fan. Rub the potatoes all over with a little olive oil and sea salt and bake on a baking tray for 60–90 mins, until crispy on the outside and soft in the middle.

2. Twenty five minutes before the potatoes are ready, make the beans. Heat the olive oil in a large frying pan over a high heat and fry the onion for 5–7 minutes, until soft and starting to caramelise.

3. Add the garlic and cherry tomatoes and fry for another couple of minutes. Stir in the ground coriander and chilli flakes, then add the black beans and hot stock.

4. Bring to the boil and simmer for 15 minutes until the stock has reduced, almost to nothing.

5. Stir in the chopped coriander and serve over the jacket potatoes with wedges of lime on the side.

Tip for tinies
Remove the chilli flakes and serve these on the side for the adults.

easy
speedy
lunches

blt: balsamic mushrooms, lettuce and tomato

This is my favourite sandwich of all time, made with rich, sticky balsamic mushrooms, juicy slices of sweet tomatoes, cashew cream, a little red onion and butter lettuce.

Serves 2

olive oil, for frying

3 large Portobello mushrooms, sliced

smooth cashew cream (page 107) or hummus

4 slices of sourdough, toasted, or other bread of your choice, such as baguette

1 large vine tomato, sliced

½ small red onion, very thinly sliced

4 lettuce leaves (I like butter lettuce)

sea salt

For the glaze

2½ tbsp thick balsamic vinegar

1 tsp maple syrup

1 garlic clove, crushed

1 tsp olive oil

1. Place a large saucepan on a medium heat and add a drizzle of olive oil and a sprinkle of salt. Once the pan is hot, add the mushrooms, spreading them evenly across the pan. Cook for 3–4 minutes on each side, until golden.

2. Meanwhile, stir the glaze ingredients together in a small bowl.

3. Once the mushrooms are golden, turn the heat up a little and pour in the glaze. Let it reduce and thicken for a minute or so, ensuring the mushrooms are nicely coated, then remove from the heat.

4. Spread a heaped tablespoon of cashew cream on to the first slice of toast, then add the mushrooms (half to each sandwich), followed by a layer of tomatoes, red onions, and 2 lettuce leaves.

harissa tofu wrap

This is one of my favourite recipes in the book; I love its simplicity and the mix of flavours. The yoghurt with fresh mint is light and creamy, while the pan-fried harissa tofu adds real depth and spice. Adding a squeeze of lemon brings it all together.

Serves 2

1 × 300g block of firm tofu

olive oil, for frying

1 lemon

3 tbsp harissa (see page 104)

2 tbsp maple syrup

2 tbsp fresh mint, finely sliced

100g coconut yoghurt

2 large handfuls of spinach, finely sliced

2 wraps or flatbreads

sea salt and black pepper

1. Cut the tofu into six long slices, about 1cm thick, then pat dry with kitchen paper.

2. Heat a drizzle of olive oil in a non-stick frying pan and add the tofu slices. Allow to cook for 4 minutes on each side, until golden and crispy.

3. Meanwhile, juice half of the lemon and mix the juice with the harissa and maple syrup in a small bowl, whisking to combine. Cut the remaining lemon half into wedges.

4. Mix the mint and yoghurt together, seasoning with salt and pepper to taste.

5. Add three quarters of the harissa and maple glaze to the pan and allow to cook until each piece of tofu is evenly coated in the mix, about 30 seconds to 1 minute.

6. Spread half the mint and yoghurt mixture onto the centre of each wrap, layer with the spinach and the glazed tofu, drizzling over any extra glaze from the pan, then top with the remaining glaze from the bowl.

7. Roll up the wraps and serve immediately with lemon wedges – a little squeeze of lemon adds great acidity.

smashed peas and broad beans on toast

The ideal 10-minute lunch. Great for busy days or as a quick snack for little ones, served either on toast or rice cakes. Plus the pea and broad bean mix makes a nice change from everyone's usual go-to of avocado toast. This is equally delicious, but higher in protein.

Serves 4

200g frozen peas

250g frozen broad beans

1 small bunch of mint leaves, finely chopped

grated zest and juice of 1 lemon

2 tbsp extra virgin olive oil, plus extra for drizzling

2 garlic cloves, crushed

2 tbsp coconut yoghurt

4 slices of sourdough bread, toasted

sea salt and black pepper

1. Place the peas and broad beans in 2 separate bowls, cover with boiling water and set aside for 5–10 minutes, until thawed.

2. Drain the broad beans and add them to a food processor.

3. Drain the peas and add them to the food processor along with the mint, lemon zest and juice, olive oil, garlic and coconut yoghurt and season well with salt and pepper.

4. Blitz for a couple of minutes until you have a chunky purée. Spread onto the toast slices and drizzle over a little extra olive oil.

Note

If you are short on time, replace the broad beans with 200g frozen edamame beans.

black beans
on toast

A different take on beans on toast, packed with flavour and nutrients. If you have any of the dukkah from page 101, a sprinkle works brilliantly on top of this.

Serves 4

1 tbsp olive oil

1 red onion, finely chopped

1 red chilli, finely chopped

small bunch of coriander, stalks and leaves separated and finely chopped

1 tsp black garlic paste

1 tsp ground cumin

½ tsp sweet smoked paprika

2 × 400g tins of black beans, drained and rinsed

squeeze of lime juice

4 slices of sourdough bread, toasted

sea salt and black pepper

To serve

coconut yoghurt

1–2 limes, cut into wedges

dukkah (see page 101; optional)

1. Place a large frying pan over a medium heat and gently warm the olive oil. Add the red onion, chilli and coriander stalks. Season well and fry for 5–6 minutes until the onion softens and begins to caramelise.

2. Stir in the black garlic paste, cumin and smoked paprika and fry for another minute before adding the beans and a good splash of water. Cook for another couple of minutes to warm through then stir in the coriander leaves and a big squeeze of lime juice.

3. Pile onto the toast and serve with some coconut yoghurt, a wedge of lime and a sprinkle of dukkah if you have any.

miso-glazed mushrooms on toast

A little lunch (or brunch) idea that I make on repeat. Portobello mushrooms are marinated in miso, thyme, garlic, spring onions and olive oil, baked with baby spinach, then piled on to chunky slices of sourdough. Simple, but perfect.

Serves 4

4 garlic cloves, peeled and finely sliced

2 spring onions, finely sliced

1 tsp fresh thyme leaves (or lemon thyme, if possible)

1 tbsp brown rice miso

4 tbsp extra virgin olive oil, plus extra to serve

8 Portobello mushrooms, thickly sliced

100g baby leaf spinach, washed and drained

4 slices sourdough bread, toasted

squeeze of lemon juice

small bunch of parsley, finely chopped

sea salt and black pepper

1. Preheat the oven to 180°C fan. Line a large baking tray with baking parchment.

2. In a bowl, mix together the garlic, spring onion, thyme, miso and olive oil. Season well with salt and pepper.

3. Place the mushrooms and spinach on a baking tray, spread them out, then pour over the miso mixture and use your hands to give everything a good mix.

4. Bake in the oven for 15 minutes, stirring halfway through.

5. Drizzle each piece of toast with a little extra virgin olive oil, then top with the mushrooms and spinach, making sure you drizzle over any cooking juices. Squeeze over a little lemon juice and scatter over the chopped parsley. Serve immediately.

speedy mushroom spread

My mum used to buy a mushroom spread from our local market every week and that really ignited a family love of recipes like these. It's a little less versatile than the herby butter bean dip, lemon and almond butter hummus or the minty pea dip (see pages 121, 118 and 116), but just as delicious. I love it spread on toast for an instant lunch, with a handful of rocket, a drizzle of olive oil and some fresh chilli.

Makes 1 bowl

2–3 tbsp olive oil

400g chestnut mushrooms, finely sliced

2 garlic cloves, finely sliced

½ tsp thyme leaves

juice of ½ lemon

1 tbsp tahini

sea salt and black pepper

1. Heat 1 tablespoon of the oil in a large frying pan and fry the mushrooms on a high heat for 4–5 minutes until they take on some colour. Make sure you don't overcrowd the pan, otherwise they will produce too much water, so you may need to do this in batches adding more olive oil to the pan for each batch.

2. Fry the garlic for a couple of minutes along with the last batch of mushrooms then transfer everything to a food processor along with the thyme, lemon juice, tahini and some salt and pepper. Blitz on a high speed for a couple of minutes until you have a purée.

everyday salad

This is the perfect go-to salad on busy days. Filled with a beautiful array
of textures and flavours, with crunchy croutons, juicy roasted tomatoes, peppers,
garlic, peppery greens, tangy mustard, and a little yoghurt for creaminess.
I've given options for various ingredients here so that you can use what you
have in the fridge to throw the salad together.

Serves 4

250g cherry tomatoes on the vine, snipped into clusters of 2–3 tomatoes

1 red, yellow, or orange pepper, deseeded and finely sliced

1 garlic clove, finely sliced

2 tbsp olive oil

1 large head of cos or romaine lettuce, or 2 heads of little gem, shredded

50g peppery salad leaves (watercress, rocket, mustard greens)

1 avocado, roughly chopped

1 × 400g tin of lentils

handful of crunchy croutons (see page 98)

small handful of sprouted salad topper or cress (optional)

sea salt and black pepper

For the dressing

6 tbsp extra virgin olive oil

2 tbsp lemon juice or apple cider vinegar

1 tbsp coconut yoghurt (optional)

1 tsp Dijon mustard

1. Preheat the oven to 190°C fan.

2. Put the cherry tomatoes, pepper slices and garlic into a baking tray, drizzle with the oil and season with salt and pepper. Roast in the oven for 20 minutes, until the tomatoes have softened slightly and the skins have split.

3. Toss together the remaining salad ingredients then whisk the dressing ingredients in a jug and pour over the salad, making sure to cover everything with the dressing.

4. Remove the tomatoes and peppers from the oven and serve the salad topped with the hot tomatoes, pepper and garlic and scrape over the cooking juices.

10-minute pea and pesto orzo

I've lost count of the number of times I've made this dish, or a variation of it, for the girls. Adding beans to the pesto makes it a complete meal, as they add lots of plant protein. I use it with orzo, pasta and stirred into rice as a speedy take on a risotto.

Serves 4

400g orzo or other short pasta

400g frozen peas

100g pine nuts, plus a few extra, toasted, to garnish (optional)

50g basil, leaves and stalks roughly chopped

2 garlic cloves, finely chopped

100ml extra virgin olive oil

1 × 400g tin of cannellini or butter beans, drained and rinsed

1 tbsp nutritional yeast

sea salt and black pepper

1. Bring a large saucepan of well salted water to the boil. Add the orzo and boil for 5 minutes then add the peas and boil for another 2–3 minutes, until the orzo is tender and the peas are cooked through.

2. While the pasta is cooking, toast the pine nuts in a dry frying pan over a high heat for a minute or so, until golden. Stir and toss them around to prevent them burning.

3. Place the toasted pine nuts, basil, garlic, olive oil, beans and nutritional yeast into a food processor and blitz for a couple of minutes until blended to a thick pesto.

4. Drain the pasta and peas and reserve about 200ml of the cooking water. Return the cooked pasta and peas to the saucepan.

5. Pour the pasta water slowly into the food processor with the motor running until you have a sauce – you may not need all of the water, so add it slowly.

6. Pour the sauce over the orzo and peas and mix well. Serve immediately scattered with some extra toasted pine nuts, if liked.

Tip for tinies
Omit the scattering of extra pine nuts for little ones.

one-pan shiitake noodle broth

This is one of my favourite lunches. I just love a rich broth with chilli, miso, rice vinegar and lime. The mushrooms, noodles, pak choi and spring onion add great texture and make it a really satisfying, hearty lunch or speedy dinner.

Serves 4

1 vegetable stock cube

2 tbsp brown rice miso

2 tsp toasted sesame oil

150g shitake mushrooms, finely sliced

1–2 tsp tamari or dark soy sauce

1 red chilli, deseeded (if you don't like it too hot) and finely chopped

2 garlic cloves, crushed

2 servings of noodles (100g each)

2 head of pak choi, quartered (optional)

juice of ½–1 lime

½ tsp rice vinegar

1 spring onion, finely sliced

sea salt (optional; there is a lot of salt in the miso and tamari)

1. Dissolve the stock cube and miso in 1 litre boiling water in a jug or bowl. Stir well and leave to one side.

2. Drizzle one teaspoon of the sesame oil into a saucepan over a medium heat. Once warm add the mushrooms and tamari. Cook for 5 minutes, until soft.

3. Remove the mushrooms and place them in a bowl to one side while you make the broth.

4. Place the saucepan back on the heat (no need to wash it up, you want to keep the mushroom flavour in there) and add the second teaspoon of sesame oil with the garlic, most of the chilli and a sprinkling of salt, if using. Sauté for 30 seconds or so, until the garlic is fragrant, then pour in the veggie broth.

5. Bring to the boil, then turn down to a simmer, add the noodles and pak choi, if using, and place the lid on the pan. Cook the noodles for as long as stated on the pack.

6. Once the noodles are soft, add the lime juice, rice vinegar and cooked mushrooms. Season to taste and add the extra teaspoon of tamari, if liked.

7. Spoon into bowls, topping each with a scattering of spring onions and the remaining chilli.

edamame, peanut and sesame noodles

Serves 4

300g flat rice noodles

300g frozen edamame beans

1 tbsp toasted sesame oil

4 spring onions, finely sliced

1 large garlic clove, finely grated

2cm piece of ginger, peeled and finely grated

1 tsp dried chilli flakes

2 tsp maple syrup

4 tsp soy sauce

juice of 1 juicy lime, 2 if it's less juicy

4 tbsp crunchy peanut butter

small bunch of coriander, leaves and stalks finely chopped

small bunch of mint, leaves roughly chopped

lime wedges, to serve

1. Bring a large saucepan of water to the boil and add the rice noodles. Cook according to the instructions on the pack, adding the edamame for the last 2 minutes, then drain and set aside.

2. Heat the sesame oil in a large wok or frying pan over a high heat. Add the spring onions, garlic, ginger and chilli flakes and fry for a minute or so.

3. Turn the heat down and stir in the maple syrup, soy sauce, lime juice and peanut butter along with 5–6 tablespoons of water.

4. Add the noodles, edamame beans, coriander and mint to the wok and give everything a good mix. I use two wooden spoons to do this so as not to break up the noodles, which are quite fragile. Add another splash of water if the sauce is too thick.

5. Once the noodles are coated in the sauce, transfer to bowls and serve immediately with lime wedges.

Tip for tinies

This is really popular with our little ones, just remove the chilli flakes and, depending on their age, swap the crunchy peanut butter for smooth, and halve or smash the edamame beans.

family favourites

tofu veggie
fried rice

Serves 4

3 tbsp toasted sesame oil

4cm piece of ginger, peeled and finely chopped

4 spring onions, finely sliced

medium bunch of coriander, stalks finely chopped, leaves reserved for garnish

1 red chilli, deseeded and finely chopped

3 carrots, peeled and finely chopped

150g sugar snap peas, mangetout or green beans, sliced

100g baby sweetcorn, sliced

200g frozen edamame beans or peas

400g cooked basmati rice (to make this quickly, you can use pre-cooked pouch)

2 × 300g blocks firm tofu, drained and patted dry

3 tbsp tamari

1 lime, to serve

sea salt and black pepper

1. Heat the sesame oil in a large wok or frying pan over a high heat. Add the ginger, spring onions, coriander stalks, chilli (if using), carrots, sugar snap peas and sweetcorn and stir fry for a few minutes until the vegetables take on some colour and soften.

2. Add the edamame beans, basmati rice and crumble in the tofu. Stir fry again for a few minutes until the edamame beans have thawed then stir in the tamari and reserved coriander leaves.

3. Taste and season as needed, squeezing lime juice over the pan before serving.

Tip for tinies
Halve or smash the edamame beans for very little ones and leave out the chilli – sprinkle it over the adult portions just before serving.

herby garlic mushrooms with butter bean mash

Don't be put off by the long ingredients list, this recipe uses the same ingredients across the three sections.

Serves 4

10 garlic cloves, crushed

1 tsp balsamic vinegar

1 tsp maple syrup

2 tbsp olive oil

12–16 large portobello mushrooms (3–4 per person, depending on their size)

sea salt

For the mash

50ml olive oil

6 garlic cloves

2 × 400g tins of butter beans, drained and rinsed

2 big handfuls of spinach

25ml unsweetened almond milk

10g flat-leaf parsley

10g coriander

½ lemon

For the herby garnish

50g flat-leaf parsley

1 garlic clove

grated zest of 1 lemon, juice of half

100ml extra virgin olive oil

1 tsp maple syrup

1. Heat the oven to 180°C fan.

2. Mix the garlic, vinegar, maple syrup and olive oil in a small bowl, seasoning with salt. Cut the stems out of the mushrooms and place the caps on a large baking tray, rounded-side up. Lightly brush the top of the mushrooms with the garlic mixture, then flip them over and coat the flat side of the mushrooms – you want lots of garlic all over them. Bake in the oven for 25 minutes.

3. Meanwhile, make the garnish and mash. For the garnish, simply put everything into a food processor and blitz for a few seconds. If you don't have a processor, simply finely chop the parsley and garlic, then combine with the remaining ingredients.

4. To make the mash, pour the olive oil into a medium frying pan and sauté the garlic with a sprinkling of salt for 2 minutes or so, then add the butter beans. Let them cook for a further 5–10 minutes, until the beans are nice and soft.

5. Place the butter bean mixture in the food processor (there's no need to wash it in between) and blitz with all the remaining mash ingredients, until smooth and creamy (you can also do this with a handheld blender, but it's not quite as creamy).

6. Place the mash on a plate, pile the mushrooms on top and drizzle with the herby garnish to finish.

Tip for tinies

Use only half the garlic.

smoky tofu tacos

These are brilliant for big family meals, or when you've got friends coming over. Having lots of bowls that everyone can pick from to assemble their own meal always works well with children I find. To make the meal even heartier, serve this with the black bean jacket potato topping (see page 204) on the side.

Serves 4

1 tbsp olive oil

½ red onion, finely sliced

150g chestnut mushrooms, finely sliced

1 garlic clove, finely sliced

1 tsp ground cumin

1 tsp dried thyme

1 × 225g pack of firm smoked tofu, drained and crumbled

150g cherry tomatoes, halved

small bunch of coriander, leaves and stalks finely chopped

sea salt and black pepper

For the quick pickled red onion

½ red onion, finely sliced

2 tbsp red wine vinegar

1 tbsp maple syrup

1 tsp sea salt

To serve

12 corn taco shells

1 avocado, finely sliced

½ iceberg lettuce, shredded

2 limes, halved

1. First make the pickled red onion. Mix all the ingredients together and leave to marinate while you make the filling.

2. To make the filling, heat the olive oil in a large frying pan over a high heat, then add the red onion and fry for 3–4 minutes, stirring occasionally so that it doesn't burn. Add the mushrooms, season well with salt and pepper, and fry for another 3–4 minutes until they have taken on some colour.

3. Stir in the garlic, cumin and thyme and fry for another minute or so before adding the crumbled tofu and cherry tomatoes. Stir fry for 4-5 minutes until the tomatoes have begun to soften a little then turn off the heat and mix in the chopped coriander.

4. Fill each taco shell with the tofu, a few slices of avocado and some shredded lettuce. Top with the pickled red onion and squeeze over lime juice to taste.

Tip for tinies

If your little ones are too young for hard taco shells serve these with soft tortillas instead.

pepper and oyster mushroom fajitas

I made a variation of these for one of our first family meals, when Skye was about 10 months old. We'd just started eating together and it was so nice to share a meal properly. We've kept making them ever since. The oyster mushrooms add a great 'meatiness' and roast beautifully, but you can swap them for another kind of mushroom, as I know they're not the easiest thing to get hold of.

Serves 4

2 red onions, 1 cut into slim wedges, 1 finely chopped

2 red peppers, halved, deseeded and sliced

1 × 400g tin of pinto or black beans, drained and rinsed

150g oyster mushrooms, cleaned, large mushrooms torn in half (or button mushrooms, if you can't get oyster)

3 garlic cloves, crushed

1½ tsp ground cumin

1½ tsp smoked paprika

1 tsp ground coriander

1 tsp chipotle paste, or to taste (optional)

2 tbsp olive oil

2 avocados, halved and stoned

juice of 2 limes

250g cherry tomatoes, quartered

handful of coriander, roughly chopped

To serve

8 corn tortillas

smooth cashew cream (see page 107)

1. Preheat the oven to 200°C fan.

2. Add the onion wedges, peppers, beans and mushrooms to a large baking tray.

3. In a small bowl, combine 2 of the crushed garlic cloves with the cumin, paprika, ground coriander, chipotle paste and olive oil. Pour the spice mix over the vegetables, season to taste and toss to ensure the veg is coated in the spice mix. Spread the veg out in a single, even layer and roast for 20–25 minutes, until the vegetables are golden and just tender.

4. Meanwhile, mash the avocado and mix with half the chopped onion and half the remaining garlic. Season and add a little of the lime juice, to taste.

5. In a separate bowl, combine the tomatoes with the remaining chopped onion and garlic. Season and add a little lime juice and coriander, to taste.

6. Warm through the tortillas and serve with the vegetables, avocado, tomato salsa and cashew cream.

Tip for tinies
Skip the chipotle paste for little ones.

root veg and black bean pie

If you're making this for toddlers, I'd leave out the miso as it's high in salt.

Serves 4–6

5g dried mushrooms

3 tbsp olive oil

1 onion, finely chopped

1 celery stick, trimmed and finely chopped

1 large carrot, peeled and grated

4 thyme sprigs

250g chestnut mushrooms, cleaned and finely chopped

4 sun-dried tomatoes, finely chopped

1 × 400g tin of chopped tomatoes

1 × 400g tin of black beans, drained and rinsed

150ml vegetable stock

250g sweet potatoes, peeled and cut into large chunks

500g floury potatoes, such as Maris Piper, peeled and cut into large chunks

250g celeriac, peeled and cut into large chunks

1 tbsp nutritional yeast

splash of oat milk

1 tsp brown rice miso

1. Pop the dried mushrooms in a cup, cover with 100ml boiling water and set aside.

2. Heat half the oil in a large saucepan. Add the onion, celery, carrot and thyme sprigs, cover and cook very gently for 10 minutes. Give the mixture a stir from time to time and add a splash of water if it looks like it might catch.

3. Once the mixture has softened, scoop it out of the pan and set aside. Add a dash more oil to the pan, add the chestnut mushrooms and cook over a medium heat for 6–8 minutes, until the mushrooms have browned and any liquid has evaporated.

4. Preheat the oven to 180°C fan.

5. Return the softened veg to the pan and stir in the sun-dried tomatoes, chopped tomatoes, beans and vegetable stock. Drain the dried mushrooms, reserving the soaking liquor. Check the liquor and strain off any grit. Add to the pan with the dried mushrooms. Bring the mixture to the boil, lower the heat and simmer gently for 25–30 minutes, until the liquid has thickened and reduced.

6. Meanwhile, add the potatoes and celeriac to a large saucepan and cover with cold water. Cover, bring to the boil and simmer for 12–15 minutes, until the vegetables are just tender. Drain well and mash with the remaining olive oil and the nutritional yeast. Add a splash of oat milk if the mash is a little thick. Season to taste.

7. Season the sauce, stir in the miso and discard the thyme sprigs. Spread the sauce out into a large baking dish (about 30 × 25cm) and spoon over the mash. Spread out and bake for 20–25 minutes, until golden and bubbling. Allow to sit for a few minutes before serving.

Paula's lentil pie

I make a big batch of the lentil ragu in this pie most weeks and use it twice during the week for quick family meals. The ragu is so versatile: I also serve it with pasta, in a veggie lasagne or as a topping for jacket potato.

Serves 4

olive oil

1 white onion (about 150g), finely chopped

2 garlic cloves, finely chopped

1 tsp ground cumin

1 tsp paprika

2 × 400g tins of chopped tomatoes

2 × 400g tins of brown lentils, drained and rinsed

sea salt and black pepper

For the topping

4 potatoes (about 800g)

225ml oat milk

2 tbsp olive oil

2 tbsp nutritional yeast

sea salt (I use ¼ teaspoon fine sea salt)

1. Preheat the oven to 160°C fan.

2. Place a large heavy-bottomed saucepan over a medium heat and fry the onion and garlic in a drizzle of olive oil for about 5 minutes, until soft. Add the spices and fry for another 2 minutes.

3. Add the chopped tomatoes. Allow to simmer, stirring occasionally for 15 minutes, or until the tomatoes have reduced slightly and become darker in colour. Season to taste (leave out salt if making for a baby under 12 months of age). Add the lentils and stir to combine.

4. Meanwhile, make the topping. Chop the potatoes into 2.5cm pieces, leaving the skin on if you like. Place in a large saucepan and cover with cold water. Bring to a gentle simmer and cook until they are fork tender and just beginning to lose their shape, about 25 minutes. Drain and allow the potatoes to dry thoroughly (if they are too wet you will have a grainy mash).

5. Heat the milk, olive oil and nutritional yeast in the same saucepan, until very gently simmering (if you add hot potatoes to cold milk you will have a gluey mash). When the potatoes are dry and they are starting to turn white at the edges place them in the pan of warm milk and mash. Add salt to taste.

6. Spread the lentils out in the base of a baking dish (about 24 × 32cm). Spread the mashed potatoes on top. If desired you can run a fork across the surface and drizzle with extra olive oil for an extra golden and crunchy topping. Bake for 40-45 minutes until golden brown and bubbling.

7. Remove from the oven and allow to cool for 10 minutes before serving.

easy veggie lasagne

This recipe is a staple in our house, especially when we've got lots of little ones coming over. It's filling, easy to prep in advance and always a hit; plus, it freezes well.

Serves 6

1½ tbsp olive oil

1 onion, peeled, halved and finely chopped

2 celery sticks, peeled and finely chopped

2 carrots, peeled and coarsely grated

250g chestnut mushrooms, peeled and finely chopped

4 garlic cloves, peeled and crushed

4 thyme sprigs

100ml red wine, or 100ml extra vegetable stock

2 tbsp tomato purée

2 × 400g tins of green lentils, drained and rinsed

2 × 400g tins of chopped tomatoes

250ml vegetable stock

12 spelt lasagne sheets

For the white sauce

4 tbsp olive oil

80g plain flour

700ml oat milk

2 bay leaves

pinch of freshly ground nutmeg

2 tbsp nutritional yeast

sea salt and black pepper

1. Heat the oil in a large saucepan and add the onion, celery and carrot. Cover and cook for 8–10 minutes, until softened. Give the vegetables an occasional stir and add a splash of water if it looks like they might catch.

2. Increase the heat slightly and add the mushrooms. Fry for 5–6 minutes, until the mushrooms have browned and the water has evaporated. Add the garlic, cook for 1 minute, then add the thyme and red wine. Allow the wine to bubble briefly before stirring in the tomato purée, lentils, chopped tomatoes and vegetable stock. Bring to the boil, lower the heat and simmer for 20–25 minutes, until thickened and reduced.

3. Preheat the oven to 160°C fan.

4. To make the white sauce, heat the oil in a large saucepan. Add the flour and cook, stirring, for 1–2 minutes, until the flour smells biscuity. Remove from the heat and gradually add the milk, stirring constantly, until smooth. Return to the heat, add the bay leaves and nutmeg and continue to stir until the sauce is bubbling and has thickened. Stir in the nutritional yeast.

5. Check the seasoning in the ragu and white sauce, and remove and discard the thyme stalks and bay leaves.

6. Spoon half the lentil ragu into a large baking dish (about 23 × 30cm) and lay over 4 of the lasagne sheets. Top with half the white sauce, followed by another layer of lasagne sheets and the final layer of ragu. Lay over the final 4 lasagne sheets and spoon over the remainder of the white sauce, smoothing it over evenly. Bake for 40–45 minutes, until golden brown on top and bubbling. Leave to stand for 5 minutes before cutting into portions.

veggie meatballs with tomato sauce

Serves 4

5g dried mushrooms

2 tbsp olive oil, plus a little extra for baking

1 large onion, peeled, halved and finely chopped

1 medium carrot, peeled and coarsely grated

2 large garlic cloves, peeled and crushed

2 tbsp tomato purée

1 × 400g tin of cannellini beans, drained and rinsed

small handful of basil leaves, roughly chopped (plus extra to serve)

1½ tbsp nutritional yeast

¼ tsp dried oregano

2 tsp tamari

75g fresh breadcrumbs

1 tsp sweet smoked paprika

1 × 400g tin of chopped tomatoes

½ tbsp balsamic vinegar

4 servings of spaghetti or other long pasta (75g per person)

1. Preheat the oven to 180°C fan and lightly oil a baking sheet. Put the mushrooms into a cup, cover with boiling water and set aside to rehydrate.

2. Heat the oil in a large saucepan. Add the onion and carrot and cook over a very low heat for 8–10 minutes, until softened. Stir the mixture occasionally and add a splash of water if it looks like it might catch.

3. Once the vegetables are soft, add the garlic and cook for 1 minute, then stir in the tomato purée and remove from the heat.

4. Drain the mushrooms and roughly chop. Blend in a food processor with half the cooked vegetables, the beans, basil, nutritional yeast, oregano, tamari and breadcrumbs to create a thick paste.

5. Using wet hands, roll the paste into 16 balls, transfer to the baking sheet and bake for 18–20 minutes, until golden and firm at the edges.

6. While the meatballs are cooking, return the saucepan to the heat and add the paprika. Cook for 1 minute, then pour in the tomatoes, half a can of water and the vinegar. Simmer for 10-12 minutes, until thickened and reduced. Season to taste.

7. Meanwhile, cook the spaghetti according to the instructions on the pack, then drain well. Toss the spaghetti in the sauce, then serve in bowls, adding the meatballs on top. Scatter over extra basil to finish.

Tip for tinies
For toddlers, skip the tamari – it's high in salt.

spring bolognese: spinach and asparagus

I love asparagus, it's one of my favourite vegetables and it really sings in this dish where it's simmered with lentils, spinach, onions, pasata and celery, then tossed with fresh basil and spaghetti. This is hearty, seasonal and just so good.

Serves 4

2 tbsp olive oil

1 onion, finely chopped

1 celery stick, finely chopped

1 × 400g tin of brown lentils, drained and rinsed

200g asparagus (or purple sprouting or Tenderstem broccoli), trimmed and roughly chopped

200g frozen spinach or baby leaf spinach

300ml hot vegetable stock

500ml passata

4 servings of spaghetti (75g per person)

20g basil, stalks and leaves finely chopped

sea salt and black pepper

1. Heat the oil in a casserole or saucepan and add the onion and celery, season well with salt and pepper, and cook over a medium heat for 5–7 minutes until soft.

2. Add the lentils, asparagus and spinach (if using fresh, you will need to do this in a couple of stages: let the first batch wilt before adding the next), stir well then pour in the hot stock. Bring to the boil and simmer for a couple of minutes.

3. Add the passata, bring back to the boil and simmer for 10–15 minutes until the asparagus is tender.

4. Meanwhile, cook the pasta according to the instructions on the pack, then drain well.

5. Stir the basil into the sauce then mix this through the spaghetti.

summer bolognese: heritage tomato

This is best made when summer tomatoes are at their finest. You could use any variety of tomatoes – I like using seasonal heritage varieties but you could also use some cherry tomatoes, salad or plum tomatoes and a few beef tomatoes. It's simple but perfect.

Serves 4

6 tbsp olive oil

6 garlic cloves, finely sliced

6 sun-dried tomatoes, finely chopped

1.2kg tomatoes of choice, roughly chopped

200g cashews

grated zest of 1 lemon

small bunch of basil, leaves and stalks finely chopped

4 servings of spaghetti or long pasta (75g per person)

sea salt and pepper

1. Heat the olive oil in a casserole or saucepan over a medium heat then add the garlic and fry for 2–3 minutes until lightly golden.

2. Stir in the sun-dried tomatoes and fry for another minute before tipping in the fresh tomatoes and plenty of salt and black pepper.

3. Mix well then bring to the boil and simmer with the lid on for 20 minutes.

4. Meanwhile, toast the cashews in a dry frying pan over a medium heat until golden, then transfer to a food processor and blitz until they resemble breadcrumbs (about 30 seconds). Set aside.

5. Check the tomato sauce: after 20 minutes the tomatoes should have softened and broken down. Turn the heat off and stir in the cashews, lemon zest and basil.

6. Cook the pasta according to the instructions on the pack, then drain well.

7. Stir the sauce through the spaghetti and serve immediately.

Note

I debated whether to peel the tomatoes, but I don't mind the skins in the sauce and felt it best to use the whole fruit rather than waste anything. If you'd rather create a smoother texture then blitz the tomato mixture in a blender before adding the cashews.

autumn bolognese: mushroom and lentil

This autumnal bolognese has lovely depth to it, with rich tones from the mushrooms and tamari, a little freshness from the parsley and a perfectly chunky texture from the lentils. It's hearty, filling, and a fantastic batch cooking recipe.

Serves 4, with extra for freezing

20g dried porcini mushrooms

300ml hot vegetable stock

1 tbsp olive oil, plus extra for frying

1 onion, finely chopped

1 celery stick, finely chopped

1 carrot, finely chopped

2 tbsp tomato purée

1 tbsp tamari or light soy sauce

500ml passata

2 × 400g tins of green lentils, drained and rinsed

400g chestnut mushrooms, finely sliced

4 servings of spaghetti (75g per person)

20g flat-leaf parsley, leaves and stalks finely chopped

sea salt and black pepper

1. Soak the dried porcini in the hot vegetable stock and set aside.

2. Meanwhile, heat the oil in a large casserole and add the onion, celery and carrot. Season with salt and pepper and cook over a medium heat for 10 minutes until soft and starting to caramelise.

3. Pour in the soaked porcini with all the stock then stir in the tomato purée and tamari. Bring to a simmer and cook for a couple of minutes before adding the passata and green lentils. Bring back to a simmer and allow to bubble away while you cook the mushrooms.

4. Heat a little oil in a non-stick frying pan and fry the mushrooms in batches on a high heat. Season each batch with salt and pepper then stir into the bubbling sauce while you fry the remaining mushrooms, until they are all cooked.

5. Cook the spaghetti according to the instructions on the pack, then drain well.

6. Stir the parsley into the sauce and check the seasoning, then add the drained spaghetti and mix well. Serve immediately.

Note
This serves 4 generously but it takes hardly any time to make so the leftovers can be frozen for another meal. Good for batch cooking, it also works brilliantly served with rice or spooned over a jacket potato.

Tip for tinies
For toddlers, skip the tamari – it's high in salt.

winter bolognese: tofu and root veg

A veggie bolognese, made with tofu instead of the usual lentils, which gives this a really nice chunky texture that's a little heartier and thicker. The rosemary, thyme, celeriac and leeks add great flavour, while the tamari gives a nice depth to the whole dish.

Serves 4, generously

1 tbsp olive oil

3 leeks, washed, trimmed and finely chopped

2 carrots, peeled and finely chopped

400g celeriac, peeled and finely diced

2 rosemary sprigs, leaves removed and finely chopped

3–4 thyme sprigs, leaves removed and finely chopped

2 tbsp tomato purée

1 tbsp tamari or dark soy sauce

450g firm tofu, drained and crumbled

300ml hot vegetable stock

500g passata

4 servings of spaghetti or other long pasta (75g per person)

1. Heat the oil in a large saucepan then stir in the leeks, carrots, celeriac, rosemary and thyme. Season well and fry on a low heat for 15-20 minutes until everything is really soft.

2. Add the tomato purée and tamari then stir in the crumbled tofu. Give everything a good mix.

3. Pour in the hot stock, bring to the boil and simmer for 5 minutes.

4. Add the passata, bring back to the boil and simmer for another 15 minutes with the lid on.

5. Meanwhile, cook the spaghetti according to the instructions on the pack and drain.

6. Stir the spaghetti into the sauce, mixing well. Serve immediately.

Notes
This freezes well so is good to cook in a large batch. The leftovers also keep well for later in the week.

Tip for tinies
For toddlers, skip the tamari – it's high in salt.

Gemma's green mac and cheese

Amazingly creamy and nutty, this dish will always leave you satisfied. This recipe includes nutritional yeast, which is a great additional source of B vitamins and it is also a complete protein.

Serves 4–6

400g macaroni

250g baby leaf spinach

25g fresh basil, roughly chopped, plus a few extra leaves to garnish

150g frozen peas

sea salt

For the sauce

100g cashews

750ml water

1 large carrot, peeled and cut into chunks

1 medium potato, peeled and cut into chunks

1 medium white onion, roughly chopped

1 celery stick, roughly chopped

3 garlic cloves, peeled and roughly chopped

1 tsp smooth Dijon mustard

8 tbsp nutritional yeast

200ml oat milk

For the topping

80g wholemeal breadcrumbs

2 tsp olive oil

1 tbsp nutritional yeast

1. Preheat the oven to 160°C fan.

2. Start by making the sauce. Put the cashews and water into a saucepan and bring to the boil. Boil fiercely for 5 minutes, then add the carrot, potato, onion and celery. Continue to simmer until all the vegetables are tender, at least 10 minutes.

3. Drain and transfer to a blender. Add all the remaining sauce ingredients and season with salt. Blend until smooth.

4. Bring a large pan of water to the boil with a pinch of salt. Add the macaroni and cook according to the packet instructions. Place the spinach in a colander, pour the macaroni into the colander over the spinach to wilt it. Drain well then place in a bowl. Add the sauce, basil and peas and mix well to combine. Pour the mixture into a 25 × 19cm baking dish.

5. For the topping, place the breadcrumbs, olive oil and nutritional yeast in a clean bowl and stir to combine. Ensure all the breadcrumbs are evenly coated in oil to ensure maximum crispiness. Sprinkle over the pasta.

6. Bake in the oven for 35–40 minutes or until dark golden brown on top. Garnish with the reserved basil leaves before serving.

instant pizza

We make these pizzas a lot and the girls absolutely love them. They're ideal for busy days when you need something quick and simple that you know everyone will eat!

Makes 4 × 20cm pizzas

280g self-raising flour, plus extra for dusting

280g coconut yoghurt

2 tbsp olive oil, plus extra to drizzle

pinch of sea salt

8 tbsp passata

Topping ideas

sliced tomato

sliced red onion

finely sliced mushrooms

finely sliced pepper

blanched broccoli florets

roasted squash pieces

drained tinned sweetcorn

olives

mushroom spread (see page 218), can be used like the passata or spooned on top in little mounds

herby butterbean dip (see page 121), can be used in place of the passata or spooned on top in little mounds

blanched, drained and chopped spinach

basil leaves

1. Preheat the oven to 200°C fan.

2. Use a wooden spoon to mix the flour, yoghurt, oil and salt together in a large mixing bowl until combined.

3. Turn the dough out onto a well-floured surface and press and pat gently to bring it together. It will be sticky, but don't worry.

4. Divide the dough into 4 equal balls. Dust the surface and each ball with more flour and roll each one into a circle, about 20cm wide.

5. Take 2 pizza bases and transfer each one on to a baking tray and bake in the oven for 3–4 minutes.

6. Remove from the oven, spread 2 tablespoons of passata onto each base then add your chosen toppings and a good drizzle of oil. Return to the oven and bake for another 8–10 minutes until the base is crispy.

Tip for tinies

The girls love getting involved in these, choosing and placing their toppings.

mushroom, lentil and pesto wheels

Stuffing rolls of puff pastry with different vegetables and pesto to make pin wheels has become a real staple in our house as it's so quick to put the together and the girls love them. Like the butter bean version on the next page, these mushroom wheels are fun for children but make a really moreish snack for adults too.

Makes 12 wheels

1 × 320g sheet of vegan puff pastry

olive oil, for frying

½ small onion, finely chopped

2 garlic cloves, finely chopped

150g mushrooms, very finely diced (the pieces should be roughly the same size as the lentils)

1 × 400g tin of green lentils, drained and rinsed

100g basil pesto (see page 112 or use store-bought)

big handful of baby spinach, finely chopped

1 tsp oat milk

1. Preheat the oven to 200°C fan. Line a baking tray with baking parchment.

2. Roll the pastry out on to the paper and place to one side.

3. Place a large frying pan over a medium heat with a drizzle of olive oil, add the onion and cook for 5 minutes, until soft. Then add the garlic and cook for a minute or so, before adding the mushrooms. Let them cook for about 5 minutes.

4. Add the lentils, pesto and spinach, cooking for a minute or so until the spinach wilts, then transfer the mix onto a plate and leave it to cool for about 10 minutes.

5. Spoon the mix evenly onto the pastry, leaving a 2.5cm strip free along the top edge. Gently pat it down. Lightly brush the pastry edge with the oat milk.

6. Roll the pastry lengthways away from you (so the strip at the top is the last part you roll), keeping it as tight as possible so that it creates a tight spiral. It should look like a big sausage roll. Make sure you seal the roll properly by firmly pressing down the strip at the top onto the pastry below.

7. Use a serrated knife to cut the log into 12 even rolls, each piece should be about 3cm wide.

8. Lay each roll, face up, on a baking tray, leaving 4–5cm between each one as they'll expand as they cook.

9. Bake for 20–25 minutes, until the pastry is golden.

butter bean, pesto and red pepper wheels

I started making these for Skye when she was really little, and they quickly became a family favourite. Adding the butter beans gives the filling a nice chunky texture and adds plant protein, turning them into a simple and delicious meal. These are our original recipe, but we've since started making the mushroom, lentil and pesto version (on page 259 and shown opposite) to mix up our weekly menus.

Makes 12 wheels

1 × 320g sheet of vegan puff pastry

olive oil, for frying

½ red onion, finely diced

2 garlic cloves, crushed

1 large sweet pointed pepper, diced

1 × 400g tin of butter beans, drained

100g almond and tomato pesto (see page 112 or use store-bought)

1 tsp oat milk

1. Pre-heat the oven to 200°C. Line a baking tray with baking parchment.

2. Roll the pastry out on to the parchment and place to one side.

3. Place a large frying pan over a medium heat with a drizzle of olive oil, add the onion and cook for 5 minutes, until soft. Then add the garlic and cook for a minute or so, before adding the pepper. Let this cook for about 5 minutes.

4. Meanwhile, either place the butter beans in a food processor and quickly blitz, or mash with a fork, then add them to the frying pan along with the pesto.

5. Stir and cook for a further 2 minutes then spoon the mix onto a plate and leave it to cool for about 10 minutes.

6. Spoon the mixture evenly onto the pastry, gently patting it down and leaving a 2.5cm strip free along the top edge. Lightly brush the edge with the oat milk.

7. Roll the pastry lengthways away from you (so the strip at the top is the last part you roll), keeping it as tight as possible so that it creates a tight spiral. It should look like a big sausage roll. Make sure you seal the roll properly by firmly pressing down the strip at the top onto the pastry below.

8. Use a serrated knife to cut the log into 12 even rolls, each piece should be about 3cm wide.

9. Lay each roll, face up, on a baking tray, leaving 4–5cm between each one as they'll expand as they cook.

10. Bake for 20–25 minutes, until the pastry is golden.

sweets

cherry and almond granola bars

These are my go-to after-nursery snack for the girls. They're packed with fibre and nourishing ingredients, they're not too sweet, nicely chewy, and relatively easy to make. I make a batch every week or so, and sometimes mix up the nut and dried fruit to vary the flavour – making them with peanut butter is absolutely delicious, too!

Makes 12

15g chia seeds

70g almonds

130g dates (unpitted weight)

20g coconut oil

40ml brown rice syrup

80g almond butter

1 teaspoon vanilla bean paste

pinch of sea salt

70g jumbo oats

70g porridge oats

60g dried cherries, halved

a few drops of almond extract (optional, but delicious!)

1. Preheat the oven to 175°C fan. Line a 20 × 20cm baking dish with baking parchment.

2. Place the chia seeds in a small bowl with 2 tablespoons of water, let them sit for 10 minutes. They'll expand, soak up the water and form a gel.

3. Place the almonds onto a baking tray and roast for 7–8 minutes until toasted, then remove and leave to cool.

4. Place the dates in boiling water and leave to soak for 5 minutes to soften. Then drain, reserving some of the water, and remove the stones.

5. Once cool, place the almonds in a small food processor and quickly pulse to break them up into small chunks. Remove and leave to one side, then blend the dates in the food processor to form a paste – you may need a teaspoon or two of their soaking water.

6. Melt the coconut oil in a small saucepan over a low heat and add the rice syrup and almond butter, stirring until smooth and creamy. Remove from the heat and stir in the vanilla and salt.

7. Pour the almonds, oats, dried cherries and almond extract into a bowl and stir to combine. Then stir in the date mix, chia gel and melted coconut oil mixture.

8. Spoon the mixture on to the baking tray, pushing it down with a spatula so that it's tightly packed. Bake for 20 minutes, then remove from the oven and leave to cool. The mixture will finish setting as it cools.

9. Cut into 12 bars and store at room temperature in an airtight container for up to 5 days.

easy berry muffins

This is a recipe that we make on repeat in our house because they're the kind of snack that everyone likes. The banana gives the muffins a lovely touch of sweetness, which is enhanced by the vanilla bean paste, and the baked berries are brilliantly juicy.

Makes 12

150g spelt flour

250g plain flour

150g coconut sugar

2 tsp baking powder

1 tsp bicarbonate of soda

pinch of sea salt

5 tbsp olive oil

1 ripe banana (about 85g), mashed

275ml oat milk

2 tsp vanilla bean paste

grated zest and juice of 1 lemon

125g blueberries

100g berries of your choice

1. Preheat the oven to 160°C fan and line a muffin tray with 12 cases. Put the spelt and plain flour, coconut sugar, baking powder, bicarbonate of soda and salt into a large mixing bowl and use a whisk to stir to combine them.

2. Add the oil, banana, milk, vanilla, lemon zest and juice to a jug and whisk to combine. Gradually add the wet ingredients to the dry, whisking as you go, until you have a smooth batter.

3. Gently fold 150g of the blueberries and berries into the batter, then divide the batter between the muffin cases. Dot the remaining blueberries and berries on top and press in lightly, so they're still poking out.

4. Bake for 20–25 minutes until golden and a skewer inserted into the centre of a muffin comes out clean. Enjoy warm or when they have cooled.

banana and olive oil loaf (no added sugar)

I make this recipe all the time for the girls, it's brilliant and they absolutely love it. It's soft and spongy and the prunes or dates make the loaf lovely and sweet – you really don't miss sugar at all. It's perfect on its own, but equally delicious as a pudding with coconut yoghurt.

Makes 1 loaf

200g self-raising flour, sifted

1 tsp baking powder

3 very ripe bananas, mashed

4 tbsp coconut yoghurt

75ml olive oil, plus extra for greasing

1 tsp vanilla bean paste

100g prunes or medjool dates, chopped

1 tbsp ground flaxseed

75g sultanas or raisins

1. Preheat the oven to 160°C fan.

2. Grease a 900g loaf tin and line with baking parchment.

3. In a large bowl, mix together the flour and baking powder.

4. In a separate bowl, mix together the banana, coconut yoghurt, olive oil, vanilla, prunes and flaxseed. Stir in the sultanas.

5. Add the banana mixture to the flour and mix well – it will seem dry at first but it will come together.

6. Pour the mixture into the loaf tin, level out the top and bake for 50–60 minutes, until risen and golden. Test with a skewer – if it comes out clean the loaf is ready.

7. Leave to cool in the tin for 15 minutes before turning out.

coconut and vanilla cupcakes

These are Skye's favourite recipe, she's been asking for them for almost a year now! The cupcakes are so quick and easy to make – the batter comes together in just five minutes or so.

Makes 12

165g self-raising flour

100g coconut sugar

40g desiccated coconut

½ tsp bicarbonate of soda

1 tsp apple cider vinegar

65ml coconut oil, melted

130ml oat milk

4 tsp vanilla bean paste

For the icing

400g coconut yoghurt

3 tbsp maple syrup

grated zest of ½ lemon

2 tbsp shredded coconut, toasted

1. Preheat the oven to 160°C fan and line a cupcake tray with 12 cases.

2. Put the flour, sugar, desiccated coconut and bicarbonate of soda into a large mixing bowl and whisk together.

3. Add the vinegar, coconut oil, oat milk and 2 teaspoons of the vanilla to a jug and whisk to combine.

4. Gradually mix the wet ingredients into the dry, stirring as you go, until you get a smooth batter.

5. Fill each cupcake case three quarters full and bake for 15–20 minutes or until golden and a skewer inserted into the centre of a cupcake comes out clean. Transfer to a wire rack to cool.

6. Meanwhile make the icing. Put the yoghurt into a large bowl and whip using a stand mixer or electric hand whisk for 5–10 minutes until thick and holding its shape. Whisk in the maple syrup, lemon zest and remaining vanilla. Either pipe the icing on to the cupcakes using a round nozzle or smooth it over the top using a palette knife. Top with the toasted shredded coconut.

the perfect cookie,
two ways

This chapter has one of each type of sweet treat – one cake, one muffin, one bar and one ice cream. I wanted each to feel classic yet versatile, something you can come back to time and again. These cookies definitely fit that bill. They're perfectly crunchy on the outside, chewy on the inside and completely addictive. I've made them two ways for you, one version has dark chocolate and sea salt, the other has cinnamon and raisins.

Makes 15 cookies

200g plain flour

70g ground almonds

200g coconut sugar

1 tsp baking powder

pinch of sea salt

60g coconut oil, melted

90ml oat milk

1 tsp vanilla bean paste

For the chocolate cookies

70g dark chocolate (70–80% cocoa solids), cut into small chunks

flaky sea salt

For the cinnamon raisin cookies

70g raisins

1 tsp ground cinnamon

1. Preheat the oven to 180°C fan and line 2 baking trays with baking parchment.

2. Mix the flour, almonds, sugar, baking powder and salt together in a large bowl. Then stir in the melted coconut oil, oat milk and vanilla to form a dough.

3. Add the dark chocolate or the raisin and cinnamon (or see Note, below) and mix well to combine.

4. With wet hands, roll the cookie dough into 15 balls (about a tablespoon of mix for each one) and divide between the two trays, making sure to leave plenty of space between them as they spread out a lot when cooking. Gently flatten them a little.

5. If you're making the salted chocolate version, sprinkle over some salt.

6. Bake in the oven for 10 minutes. Remove from the oven and leave to cool on the tray. They'll finish setting while they cool. I think they're most delicious about an hour later when they're perfectly chewy.

7. Once cool, store in an airtight container at room temperature for up to 5 days.

Note

You can split the batch of dough in half and make some of each version. Just be sure to half the quantity of the chocolate or raisin ingredients you add to each batch.

easy chocolate cake

Don't be put off by the suggestion to use the liquid from a tin of chickpeas in this recipe. Chickpea water is often used in plant-based baking recipes in place of egg whites as it creates the same light, fluffy texture. It has to be the water from a tin; you can't get the same effect by using the water from boiling dried chickpeas.

Serves 12

400g plain flour

60g potato starch

2 tsp baking powder

1 tsp bicarbonate of soda

½ tsp fine sea salt

50g cacao powder

275g coconut sugar

115ml liquid from 1 × 400g tin of chickpeas

¼ tsp cream of tartar

3 tsp apple cider vinegar

300ml oat milk

2 tsp vanilla bean paste

200ml vegetable oil

For the icing

600g coconut yoghurt

4 tbsp cacao powder, plus extra to dust

4 tbsp maple syrup

1 tsp vanilla bean paste

1. Preheat the oven to 160°C fan and line two 20cm sandwich tins with baking parchment. Put the flour, potato starch, baking powder, bicarbonate of soda, salt, cacao and sugar into a large bowl and mix to combine.

2. In a separate bowl, whisk the chickpea liquid and cream of tartar with an electric whisk for 8–10 minutes on a medium speed until it starts to become thick and foamy like a meringue and holds its shape.

3. Whisk the vinegar, milk, vanilla and oil together in a jug. Gradually stir the wet ingredients into the dry ingredients along with a third of the whisked chickpea mixture to slacken the mixture slightly, then fold in the rest of the whisked chickpea mixture until fully combined.

4. Divide the batter evenly between the two tins and level the tops. Bake for 35 minutes or until a skewer inserted in the centre of the cakes comes out clean. Leave to cool in the tin for 5 minutes and then turn out onto a cooling rack, inverted so that the tops of the cakes are facing down (this will help to level them), and leave to cool completely.

5. Meanwhile make the icing. Put the yoghurt into a large bowl and whip using a stand mixer or electric hand whisk for 5–10 minutes, until thick and holding its shape. Add the cacao, maple and vanilla and whisk for a further minute.

6. Once the cakes are cool, level the tops using a serrated knife if necessary. Spread half of the icing over one of the cakes and sandwich it together with the other. Spread the remaining icing over the top using a palette knife if you have one to smooth it – it doesn't need to be perfect. Dust some cacao over the top of the cake to finish.

apple and berry pie

This is a beautifully vibrant pie that's absolutely worth the effort. Not only is it delicious, it looks fantastic too, with rich hues of deep purple oozing onto each plate.

Serves 4–8

coconut oil, to grease the dish

2 × Bramley cooking apples (about 500g), peeled, cored and roughly chopped

1 tsp vanilla bean paste

finely grated zest and juice of 1 lemon

500g frozen berries

120g coconut sugar

¼ tsp ground cardamom (from about 5 pods) or ¼ tsp allspice

1 tbsp cornflour

plain flour, to dust

500g vegan shortcrust pastry

plant milk, to seal the pastry

coconut yoghurt or ice cream, to serve

1. Preheat the oven to 180°C fan. Lightly grease a 20cm springform cake tin or a pie dish with coconut oil.

2. Put the apples, vanilla, lemon zest and juice into a saucepan, along with 2 tablespoons of water and mix well. Bring to the boil then cover with a lid and turn down the heat. Cook for 10 minutes until the apple has mostly broken down.

3. Remove the lid, turn up the heat and stir in the frozen berries, coconut sugar, cardamom or allspice and cornflour. Bring to the boil and simmer for a minute (this will help the cornflour to thicken the sauce). Set aside to cool while you prepare the pastry – the filling needs to cool a little so that it's not piping hot when you add it to the pastry.

4. On a floured surface, roll out two thirds of the pastry until it's big enough to line the cake tin or pie dish. Carefully press the pastry inside and up the sides of the tin, leaving the excess pastry to hang over the sides. Chill in the fridge while you make the pie lid.

5. Roll out the remaining third of pastry so it is 2cm wider than the diameter of the cake tin.

6. Pour the filling into the tin. Brush the edges with a little milk and lay the pastry lid on top. Crimp the edges to seal, then brush the entire lid with more milk.

7. Cut a little hole in the centre of the pie to allow the steam to escape and bake for 25–30 minutes, until golden.

8. Remove from the oven and leave the pie to rest in the tin for 10 minutes before serving in big slices with coconut yoghurt or ice cream.

Note

Cardamom can be fiddly to prepare and isn't widely available in ground form, but you can swap it for allspice. This is best eaten fresh on the day it's made but you can keep it in the fridge for up to 2 days. It can be eaten cold, but I'd suggest gently reheating it in a low oven.

banana ice cream with pecan brittle and chocolate chips

Makes about 600g

3 bananas (about 300g), finely sliced

70g coconut sugar

70g pecans

150ml plant milk of choice

1 tsp vanilla extract

1 tbsp maple syrup, plus extra to drizzle

pinch of salt

60g dark chocolate chips

1. Freeze the banana slices in a single layer for about 1.5–2hrs until firm.

2. Melt the coconut sugar with a tablespoon of hot water in a small saucepan over a low-medium heat for a minute, swirling the pan around as it melts (but don't stir it). Make sure all the sugar granules have dissolved, then add the pecans, stirring them in to coat them in the melted sugar.

3. Pour onto a non-stick baking mat or a sheet of baking parchment and leave to cool.

4. Once cool, break into pieces and transfer to a food processor. Blitz until you have small pieces then set aside.

5. Put the frozen bananas, plant milk, vanilla extract, maple syrup and salt into a food processor and blitz until smooth, pausing occasionally to break up any clumps.

6. Transfer the ice cream to a container and stir through the pecan praline and chocolate chips. Place back into the freezer for another couple of hours then serve in large scoops with an extra drizzle of maple syrup.

Note

Coconut sugar is darker than white sugar, so this caramel has a deeper tone. If the pan is hard to clean after making the caramel, fill it with room temperature water and bring to the boil; this will dissolve the sticky bits.

references

introduction
1. www.bda.uk.com/resource/are-we-achieving-5-a-day.html, accessed 14 Feb 2022
2. academic.oup.com/ije/article/46/3/1029/3039477, accessed 14 Feb 2022
3. bmjopen.bmj.com/content/9/10/e027546; bmjopen.bmj.com/content/6/3/e009892, accessed 14 Feb 2022
4. www.who.int/news-room/fact-sheets/detail/noncommunicable-diseases, accessed 14 Feb 2022
5. doi.org/10.3390/nu6062131, accessed 14 Feb 2022
6. doi.org10.1080/10408398.2016.1138447, accessed 14 Feb 2022
7. www.ahajournals.org/doi/10.1161/JAHA.119.012865, accessed 16 May 2022
8. academic.oup.com/ajcn/article/89/5/1627S/4596952, accessed 16 May 2022
9. www.cambridge.org/core/journals/proceedings-of-the-nutrition-society/article/longterm-health-of-vegetarians-and-vegans/263822873377096A7BAC4F887D42A4CA, accessed 16 May 2022
10. doi.org/10.3390/su11154110, accessed 16 May 2022
11. doi.org/10.1093/advances/nmz019doi.org/10.1126/science.aaq0216, accessed 16 May 2022
12. link.springer.com/article/10.1007%2Fs10584-014-1169-1, accessed 16 May 2022
13. www.nature.com/articles/s41586-018-0594-0, accessed 16 May 2022

our top 10 FAQs
1. Allès, B., Baudry, J., Méjean, C., Touvier, M., Péneau, S., Hercberg, S. & Kesse-Guyot, E. (2017). Comparison of sociodemographic and nutritional characteristics between self-reported vegetarians, vegans, and meat-eaters from the nutrinet-santé study. Nutrients, 9(9), 1023. doi: 10.3390/nu9091023.; Clarys, P., Deliens, T., Huybrechts, I., Deriemaeker, P., Vanaelst, B., & De Keyzer, W., et al. (2014). Comparison of nutritional quality of the vegan, vegetarian, semi-vegetarian, pesco-vegetarian and omnivorous diet. *Nutrients*, 6(3), 1318–1332. doi.org/10.3390/nu6031318; Sobiecki, J., Appleby, P., Bradbury, K. & Key, T. (2016). High compliance with dietary recommendations in a cohort of meat eaters, fish eaters, vegetarians, and vegans: results from the European prospective investigation into cancer and nutrition–oxford study. *Nutrition Research*, 36(5), 464–477. doi.org/10.1016/j.nutres.2015.12.016
2. www.ncbi.nlm.nih.gov/pmc/articles/PMC6899614/, accessed 25 Feb 2022; www.nature.com/articles/s41598-018-36890-3, accessed 25 Feb 2022

why the future needs to look different
1. pubmed.ncbi.nlm.nih.gov/28523941/, accessed 25 Feb 2022
2. lifestylemedicine.org/What-is-Lifestyle-Medicine, accessed 16 May 2022

what is a healthy diet?
1. www.who.int/news-room/fact-sheets/detail/noncommunicable-diseases, accessed 25 Feb 2022
2. Katz, D.L. *et al.* (2018) 'Lifestyle as Medicine: The Case for a True Health Initiative', *American Journal of Health Promotion*. doi: 10.1177/0890117117705949.
3. GBD 2017 Diet Collaborators (2019) 'Health effects of dietary risks in 195 countries, 1990–2017: a systematic analysis for the Global Burden of Disease Study 2017', *Lancet.* Published Online April 3, 2019 http://dx.doi.org/10.1016/S0140-6736(19)30041–8

4. Li, Y. *et al.* (2018) 'Impact of Healthy Lifestyle Factors on Life Expectancies in the US Population', *Circulation.* doi: 10.1007/s00402-002-0412-9.
5. Kvaavik, E. *et al.* (2010) 'Influence of individual and combined health behaviours on total and cause-specific mortality in men and women: The United Kingdom Health and Lifestyle Survey', *Archives of Internal Medicine.* doi: 10.1001/archinternmed.2010.76.

building a balanced plant-based diet
1. National Institute for Health and Care Excellence (NICE). Polycystic Ovary Syndrome Causes [Internet]. 2018 [cited 2021 Nov 4]. Available from: cks.nice.org.uk/topics/polycystic-ovary-syndrome/background-information/causes/
2. Royal College of Obstetricians and Gynaecologists. Long-Term Consequences of Polycystic ovary syndrome. 2014 [cited 2021 Nov 4]; Available from: www.rcog.org.uk/globalassets/documents/guidelines/gtg_33.pdf
3. Monash University MA. PCOS Evidence-Based guidelines [Internet]. 2018 [cited 2021 Nov 4]. Available from: www.monash.edu/__data/assets/pdf_file/0004/1412644/PCOS_Evidence-Based-Guidelines_20181009.pdf
4. Lim SS, Hutchison SK, van Ryswyk E, Norman RJ, Teede HJ, Moran LJ. Lifestyle changes in women with polycystic ovary syndrome. Cochrane Database of Systematic Reviews. 2019 Mar 28;2019(3).
5. Who.int. 2022. The top 10 causes of death. [online] Available at: www.who.int/news-room/fact-sheets/detail/the-top-10-causes-of-death, accessed 15 Feb 2022
6. Rock, C.L. *et al.* American Cancer Society guideline for diet and physical activity for cancer prevention. *CA. Cancer J. Clin.* (2020). doi:10.3322/caac.21591
7. www.lifestylemedicine.org/ACLM/About/What_is_Lifestyle_Medicine/ACLM/About/What_is_Lifestyle_Medicine_/Lifestyle_Medicine.aspx?hkey=26f3eb6b-8294-4a63-83de-35d429c3bb88, accessed 15 Feb 2022
8. GBD Diet Collaborators. Health effects of dietary risks in 195 countries, 1990–2017: a systematic analysis for the Global Burden of Disease Study 2017. Lancet Published, (2019)
9. Satija, A., Bhupathiraju, S.N., Spiegelman, D., Chiuve, S.E., Manson, J.E., Willett, W., Rexrode, K.M., Rimm, E. B., & Hu, F.B. (2017). Healthful and Unhealthful Plant-Based Diets and the Risk of Coronary Heart Disease in U.S. Adults. Journal of the American College of Cardiology, 70(4), 411–422. doi.org/10.1016/j.jacc.2017.05.047, accessed 16 May 2022
10. Barnard, N.D., Cohen, J., Jenkins, D.J., Turner-McGrievy, G., Gloede, L., Green, A., & Ferdowsian, H. (2009). A low-fat vegan diet and a conventional diabetes diet in the treatment of type 2 diabetes: a randomized, controlled, 74-wk clinical trial. The American journal of clinical nutrition, 89(5), 1588S–1596S. doi.org/10.3945/ajcn.2009.26736H
11. Rock, C.L., Thomson, C., Gansler, T., Gapstur, S.M., McCullough, M.L., Patel, A.V., Andrews, K.S., Bandera, E.V., Spees, C.K., Robien, K., Hartman, S., Sullivan, K., Grant, B.L., Hamilton, K.K., Kushi, L.H., Caan, B.J., Kibbe, D., Black, J.D., Wiedt, T.L., McMahon, C., Sloan, K. and Doyle, C. (2020), American Cancer Society guideline for diet and physical activity for cancer prevention. CA A Cancer J Clin, 70: 245–271. doi.org/10.3322/caac.21591, accessed 16 May 2022
12. 2019. UK Chief Medical Officers' Physical Activity Guidelines. [online] Available at: assets.publishing.service.gov.uk/government/uploads/system/uploads/attachment_data/

file/832868/uk-chief-medical-officers-physical-activity-guidelines.pdf, accessed 15 Feb 2022

13. Wen, C.P., Wai, J.P., Tsai, M.K., Yang, Y.C., Cheng, T.Y., Lee, M.C., Chan, H.T., Tsao, C.K., Tsai, S.P., & Wu, X. (2011). Minimum amount of physical activity for reduced mortality and extended life expectancy: a prospective cohort study. Lancet (London, England), 378(9798), 1244–1253. doi.org/10.1016/S0140-6736(11)60749-6

14. Mental health Foundation UK. Stress and Coping. 2021 [cited 2021 Nov 7]; www.mentalhealth.org.uk/news/stressed-nation-74-uk-overwhelmed-or-unable-cope-some-point-past-year

15. Bagnardi, V., Rota, M., Botteri, E., Tramacere, I., Islami, F., Fedirko, V., Scotti, L., Jenab, M., Turati, F., Pasquali, E., Pelucchi, C., Galeone, C., Bellocco, R., Negri, E., Corrao, G., Boffetta, P., & La Vecchia, C. (2015). Alcohol consumption and site-specific cancer risk: a comprehensive dose-response meta-analysis. British journal of cancer, 112(3), 580593. doi.org/10.1038/bjc.2014.579, accessed 16 May 2022

16. Alcohol Change UK. Alcohol in the UK. 2021 [cited 2021 Nov 7]; Available from: alcoholchange.org.uk/alcohol-facts/fact-sheets/alcohol-statistics

17. National Institute for Health and Care Excellence (NICE). Insomnia [Internet]. 2021 [cited 2021 Nov 7]. Available from: cks.nice.org.uk/topics/insomnia/references/

raising plant-based children

1. The Vegan Society UK www.vegansociety.com/news/media/statistics/worldwide, accessed 18 Mar 2022

2. British Dietetic Association confirms well-planned vegan diets can support healthy living in people of all ages. British Dietetic Association, 7th August 2017. Available at: www.bda.uk.com/news/view?id=179, accessed 16 May 2022

3. Nourish: The Definitive Plant-Based Nutrition Guide for Families. Reshma Shah MD, MPH and Brenda Davis RD. 2020

4. Melina V, Craig W, Levin S. Position of the Academy of Nutrition and Dietetics: Vegetarian Diets. J Acad Nutr Diet. 2016;116:1970–1980.

5. Renda M, Fischer P. Vegetaian diets in children and adolescents. Pediatr Rev. 2009; 30(1): e1-e8

6. Health Canada *Eating well with Canada's Food Guide*. www.hc-sc.gc.ca/fn-an/food-guide-aliment/index-eng.php, accessed 16 May 2022

7. Dietitians of Canada- Healthy Eating Guidelines for Vegans www.dietitians.ca/Downloads/Factsheets/Guidlines-for-Vegans.aspx, accessed 16 May 2022

8. Keller et al. 2019. Energy, Macronutrient Intake, and Anthropometrics of Vegetarian, Vegan, and Omnivorous Children (1–3 Years) in Germany (VeChi Diet Study) *Nutrients* 2019, *11*, 832; doi:10.3390/nu11040832

9. Keller et al 2021. Nutrient Intake and Status of German Children and Adolescents Consuming Vegetarian, Vegan or Omnivore Diets: Results of the VeChi Youth Study *Nutrients* 2021, *13*, 1707. pubmed.ncbi.nlm.nih.gov/34069944/, accessed 16 May 2022

10. www.bda.uk.com/resource/iodine.html, accessed 18 Mar 2022

11. www.vegansociety.com/resources/nutrition-and-health/life-stages/under-fives, accessed 18 Mar 2022

12. Nancy F Butte and Janet C King 2005. Energy requirements during pregnancy and lactation. Public Health Nutrition: 8(7A), 1010–1027

13. Dietary Reference Values: A Guide. Department of Health 1991 assets.publishing.service.gov.uk/government/uploads/system/uploads/attachment_data/file/743790/Dietary_Reference_Values_-_A_Guide__1991_.pdf, accessed 16 May 2022

14. www.biodidoo.com/premiriz-baby-milk-0-6-months-600g-premibio-a1378-en.html, accessed 16 May 2022

15. Testa et al 2018 Soy-based infant formula: Are phytoestrogens still in doubt? *Frontiers in Nutrition* 5:110 www.ncbi.nlm.nih.gov/pmc/articles/PMC6265372/

16. Vandenplas et al. Safety of soya-based infant formulas in children. *Br J Nutr.*2014;111:1340–60

17. www.smahcp.co.uk/formula-milk/soya-infant-formula, accessed 16 May 2022

18. Plant Based Nutrition course. University of Winchester. Lecture on 'Plant-based diets for babies and children' by Dr Miriam Martinez-Biarge, Paediatrician.

19. Agostoni C et al (2006): Soy protein infant formulae and follow-on formulae: a commentary by the ESPGHAN Committee on Nutrition. J Pediatr Gastroenterol Nutr, 42(4): 352–361

20. www.nhs.uk/start4life/baby/baby-vitamins/, accessed 16 May 2022

21. www.nhs.uk/conditions/baby/breastfeeding-and-bottle-feeding/breastfeeding-and-lifestyle/diet/, accessed 16 May 2022

22. Feeding your Vegan Baby: The First Year by Dr Miriam Martinez-Biarge, Paediatrician. Plant Based Health Professionals UK factsheet plantbasedhealthprofessionals.com/factsheets

23. kidshealth.org/en/parents/growth-6mos.html#catgrowth, accessed 16 May 2022

24. Great Ormond Street Hospital for Children NHS Foundation Trust. Nutritional requirements for children in health and disease, 2014

25. Shashiraj, Faridi, M., Singh, O. *et al.* Mother's iron status, breastmilk iron and lactoferrin – are they related?. *Eur J Clin Nutr* 60, 903–908 (2006). doi.org/10.1038/sj.ejcn.1602398, accessed 16 May 2022

26. Hallberg et al 1989, The role of vitamin C in iron absorption. *Int J Vitam Nutr Res Suppl* 1989;30:103–8.

27. Higher Bioaccessibility of Iron and Zinc from Food Grains in the Presence of Garlic and Onion. Smita Gautam, Kalpana Platel, and Krishnapura Srinivasan. Journal of Agricultural and Food Chemistry 2010 58 (14), 8426–8429.

28. Feeding your Vegan Baby: The Second Year by Dr Miriam Martinez-Biarge, Paediatrician. Plant Based Health Professionals UK factsheet plantbasedhealthprofessionals.com/factsheets, accessed 16 May 2022

29. kidshealth.org/en/parents/grow12yr.html#catgrowth, accessed 16 May 2022

30. Das et al Nutrition in adolescents: physiology, metabolism, and nutritional needs. *Ann N Y Acad Sci* 2017; 1393(1):21–23)

31. www.nhs.uk/conditions/vitamins-and-minerals/vitamin-d/, accessed 16 May 2022

32. The UK Iodine Group www.ukiodine.org/iodine-food-fact-sheet/, accessed 16 May 2022

33. www.bda.uk.com/resource/iodine.html, accessed 16 May 2022

34. The Relationship of Docosahexaenoic Acid (DHA) with Learning and Behavior in Healthy Children: A Review Connye N. Kuratko, Erin Cernkovich Barrett, Edward B. Nelson 1 and Norman Salem, Jr. *Nutrients* 2013, 5, 2777–2810

35. Maternal DHA Status during Pregnancy Has a Positive Impact on Infant Problem Solving: A Norwegian Prospective Observation Study. KM Stormark et al. *Nutrients* 2018, 10, 529; doi:10.3390/nu10050529

36. Plant Based Health Professionals UK plantbasedhealthprofessionals.com/vegan-supplements-for-children, accessed 16 May 2022

37. Picky eating during childhood: A longitudinal study to age 11- years. Mascola et al. *Eat Behav.* 2010 December; 11(4): 253–257. doi:10.1016/j.eatbeh.2010.05.006.

38. Picky/fussy eating in children: Review of definitions, assessment, prevalence and dietary intakes. Emmett PM et al. Appetite 95 (2015) 349e359

39. Essential Nutrients for Bone Health and a Review of their Availability in the Average North American Diet. CT Price et al. *The Open Orthopaedics Journal*, 2012, 6, 143–149

40. Soy food Intake during Adolescence and Subsequent Risk of Breast Cancer among Chinese Women Xiao Ou Shu et al. *Cancer Epidemiology, Biomarkers & Prevention* Vol. 10, 483–488, May 2001

41. Repeated exposure and conditioning strategies for increasing vegetable liking and intake: systematic review and meta-analyses of the published literature. KM Appleton et al. *The American Journal of Clinical Nutrition*, Volume 108, Issue 4, October 2018, Pages 842–856

index

about the author

Ella Mills is the founder of deliciously ella, a plant-based food and wellness platform dedicated to sharing delicious ways to feel better. She is an award-winning author and an advocate of healthy, plant-based living.

Following her own experience of ill health in 2011, Ella started the popular recipe website, deliciouslyella.com, as she learnt to cook delicious, natural, plant-based food. Ever committed to helping others enjoy this approach to cooking, Ella started a series of plant-based cooking classes and supper clubs the following year. As the website grew, Ella launched a recipe app, before writing the fastest selling debut cookbook in the UK in early 2015. Her first book, deliciously ella, went on to become a *Sunday Times* number 1 best seller, a *New York Times* best seller and has been translated into almost 30 languages. She has since released a further five best-selling books, selling over a million copies of her books in the UK alone, and amassed a social media audience of over three million people, with a popular podcast that's had a further twenty-five million downloads.

Ella has been working with her husband, Matthew, since shortly after the publication of her first book. Ella is the founder and brand director of the company; Matthew is the CEO. The office is based in central London and they've grown the company to a current team of fifty people. Together they have opened a restaurant, Plants, in London, where they demonstrate the breadth of plant-based cooking, serving everything from homemade cultured (vegan) butter to pan-fried oyster mushroom scallops with carrot jelly, confit delica pumpkin with whipped cashew cream and chocolate babka dipped in oat milk and served with homemade chocolate chip ice cream.

They have also launched multiple ranges of natural, plant-based food products, including snacks, cereals, veggie chips and soups, into thousands of stores across the UK. The brand is bought by millions of households in the UK and is set to launch internationally across Europe and the US throughout 2022 and 2023.

Ella and Matthew also run a holistic wellbeing app, feel better, which includes almost 1,000 recipes, meditation classes, sleep support and movement classes, from yoga to cardio, Pilates and barre.

Ella lives in London with her husband, Matthew, their daughters, Skye and May, and their dog, Austin.

acknowledgements

Ten years ago, deliciously ella was in many ways a pseudonym, the boundaries between person and brand were blurred and often hard to distinguish. It remained that way for the first few years, and for the first few cookbooks. Each year since Ella Mills and deliciously ella have become further separated, as deliciously ella came to represent so much more than me, it was no longer a pseudonym but a collective. First it was me plus one or two team members, one of whom is now a best friend and godmother to May, alongside a relatively small online community. Then Matthew, my husband, joined as our CEO and really my co-founder (although he's too humble to let anyone call him that), our community expanded, both across the globe and from online to offline, as we opened our cafes and started launching our food products. Now team deliciously ella is more than 50 people, plus a wonderful group of people – our experts and the fantastic freelancers who worked on the project, who collectively have bought this book to life and that's who I'd like to thank, although I could never do justice to all they do in just one page.

Shireen, Gemma, Alan, Rosie, Rohini, Paula and Shahroo, for sharing their expertise and hard-earned knowledge with us through their brilliant contributions. Louise, our brilliant designer who has bought deliciously ella to life for years now and who designed this book so beautifully. You've outdone yourself on each of the books we've done together. Louise, Emily, Orfhlaith, Ananda and Liberty who have helped bring the recipes together, testing them so thoroughly and ensuring they're exactly as they should be for you – their collectively creativity has been instrumental to this project. Imogen, the most trustworthy, insightful editor you could ask for, who has bought it all together so seamlessly. Frankie, Hannah and Clare for such a brilliant few weeks of shooting and taking the time to ensure each photo and dish looked its absolute best.

Liz and Cathryn, for trusting me since day one. I'm incredibly proud to say that of the six books we've published, I truly think this one is the best, and I'm sure it's because the dream team are back together.

And most of all to my family – Matthew, Skye and May – my whole world. Thank you for encouraging me, supporting me and truly being the foundation of my life. The home you've given me, the stability and the love, give me the confidence to chase dreams I never would have dared to. Thank you.

First published in Great Britain in 2022
by Yellow Kite Books
An Imprint of Hodder & Stoughton
An Hachette UK company

1

A CIP catalogue record for this title is available from the British Library

Hardback ISBN 978 1 529 31377 2
eBook ISBN 978 1 529 31526 4

Publisher: Liz Gough
Editor: Imogen Fortes
Creative direction: deliciously ella
Page layout: Nicky Barneby
Food photography: Clare Winfield
Portrait photography: Sophia Spring
Food styling: Frankie Unsworth
Food styling assistant: Sarah Vassallo
Prop styling: Hannah Wilkinson
Production controller: Diana Talyanina

Colour origination by Alta Image London
Printed and bound in Germany by Mohn Media

Yellow Kite
Hodder & Stoughton Ltd
Carmelite House
50 Victoria Embankment
London EC4Y 0DZ

www.yellowkitebooks.co.uk
www.hodder.co.uk
www.deliciouslyella.com

You can download all the recipes in this book on to the deliciously ella app, feel better.

The app has over 800 recipes, so you'll have a huge selection once you put the two together. To download, simply:

- make sure you have the latest version from the App Store or Google Play
- scan the QR code opposite

If you don't already have the feel better app, this QR code will take you straight to the download page where you can subscribe. Simply scan this code again to unlock the recipes in your app.

If you enjoyed this book, you might be interested in other Deliciously Ella titles.

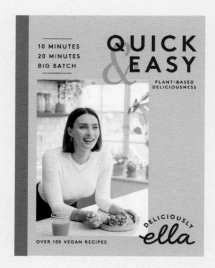

 @deliciouslyella

 @DeliciouslyElla

 /DeliciouslyElla